Carson-Dellosa Publishing

FEBRUARY

Make the Most of Every Month with Carson-Dellosa's Monthly Books!

Production Manager
Chris McIntyre

Editors
Hank Rudisill
Kelly Gunzenhauser
Carol Layton
Maria McKinney

Art Directors
Alain Barsony
Penny Casto

Illustrators
Courtney Bunn
Mike Duggins
Erik Huffine
Kelly Johnson
Amber Kocher Crouch
David Lackey
Ray Lambert
Bill Neville
Betsy Peninger
Dez Perrotti
J.J. Rudisill
Pam Thayer
Julie Webb

Cover Design
Amber Kocher Crouch
Ray Lambert
J.J. Rudisill

Carson-Dellosa Publishing Company, Inc.

FEBRUARY

Table of Contents

FEBRUARY TEACHER TIPS

LOVE

Marker Keeper
Put an end to lost marker caps with this unique marker holder. Pour plaster of paris into a bowl. Tightly place the caps on several markers and push them cap-first into the plaster of paris, then allow the mixture to dry and harden. When students need to use markers, they pull them from the holder, leaving the caps in the plaster of paris. Students can push the markers back into the matching caps after use.

Worksheet Originals
Keep track of original copies of worksheets and other handouts when making duplicates. Draw a line with a yellow highlighter across the top of the original document. The highlighter will not show up on the copies and it will remind you not to accidentally pass out your original documents.

Student Helpers
Help absent students keep up with assignments by asking the child who sits beside him to be responsible for gathering the necessary work. Have this student write down the day's assignments and collect papers and books the absent student needs. At the end of the day, have the helper take the materials to the office to be picked up.

Class Valentine List
Let students help you make a class list of names for Valentine cards. Route a sheet of lined paper and instruct each student to write her name in her best writing. Make copies of the list for students to take home as a reference for addressing Valentine cards and other correspondence.

Positive Calls Home
A positive call from school is sure to brighten a parent's day! Schedule time each month to make telephone calls to each student's parent or guardian to discuss incidents of good behavior, special achievements, and particular areas of improvement.

Computer Experts
Choose three students to act as "computer experts." Show these students how to use computer programs, operate printers, clear paper jams, etc. Let them answer questions and help their classmates whenever computer problems arise.

February

Day-by-Day Calendar

1 *American Music Month* Set up a music center with a tape recorder, headphones, and several tapes of American composers and musicians. Include a variety of musical styles including jazz, classical, and modern. Let students visit the center during freetime.

2 *Laugh and Grow Rich Day* Let students draw pictures of things that make them laugh. Then, let them share their pictures with the class.

3 *Norman Rockwell's Birthday* The painter was born on this day in 1894. He often painted everyday situations in a humorous way. Show examples of his work, then have students paint or draw their own Rockwell-style pictures entitled *A Day at School*.

4 *Charles Lindbergh's Birthday* The pilot was born on this day in 1902. Have students write journal entries about places they would travel if they were pilots.

5 *National Cherry Month* Cherries are preserved in a number of ways. Bring in maraschino cherries, canned cherries, and fresh cherries for students to sample. Have students vote for their favorites and graph the results.

6 *Compliment Day*© Have students pay compliments to their classmates.

7 *Humpback Whale Awareness Month* Teach the class facts about these animals, such as, they are the largest mammals and they have the biggest flippers of all whales.

8 *Random Acts of Kindness Week* is February 8-14. Brainstorm a list of random acts of kindness that can be done for those at school. Do something every day this week.

9 The *U.S. National Weather Service* was *established* on this day in 1870. Have students draw pictures of themselves dressed for their favorite kinds of weather. Display the pictures in groups on a bulletin board.

10 The *first singing telegram* was *delivered* on this day in 1933. Have students choose an occasion and write a singing telegram to celebrate.

11 *National Library Lovers' Month* Take the class to the school library and allow them to get acquainted with all it has to offer.

12 *Abraham Lincoln's Birthday* Tell students that Abraham Lincoln was also known by the nickname Honest Abe. Have each child pick out nicknames to suit her character.

13 *Get A Different Name Day* Pass out nametags and allow each student to choose a new name to use all day long.

14 *Great American Pies Month* Have students create recipes for the ultimate pies. The goal is not to write a "real" recipe, but to be creative. What is the ultimate flavor combination? Pizza and ice cream? Corn chips and chocolate?

15 *Campbell's® Soup* was *advertised for the first time* today in 1899. Draw and cut out a paper bowl for each student. Have students decorate the bowls like their favorite flavors of soup using supplies like yarn for noodles and construction paper for vegetables. Hang the bowls on a bulletin board.

16 *Potato Lover's Month* Bring in a variety of chips and have a potato chip party. Have students brainstorm all the foods they have eaten which contain potatoes.

17 *Michael Jordan's Birthday* The basketball player was born today in 1963. Have students write or tell what they would like to be able to do better than anyone else.

18 The planet *Pluto* was *discovered* today in 1930 by Clyde Tombaugh. Have students draw pictures of what they think life would be like on Pluto.

19 *International Embroidery Month* Show students how to do a simple cross stitch. Have them draw designs on cloth squares and sew them with blunt needles and yarn.

20 *National Wild Bird Feeding Month* Make bird feeders from empty soda bottles and twine and hang them where they are visible outside the classroom or let students take them home.

21 *International Friendship Week* is February 21-27. Have students write letters or e-mail messages to pen pals in other countries.

22 *Popcorn* was *introduced to the colonists* by Quadequina Native Americans today in 1630. Pop different flavors and share.

23 *Woody Guthrie wrote* **This Land is Your Land** today in 1940. Have the class sing this song to honor the occasion.

24 *Wihelm Grimm's Birthday* The writer was born on this day in 1786. Share a story from *Grimm's Fairy Tales* with the class.

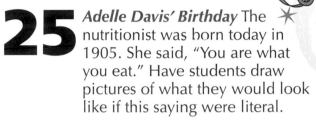

25 *Adelle Davis' Birthday* The nutritionist was born today in 1905. She said, "You are what you eat." Have students draw pictures of what they would look like if this saying were literal.

26 *American Heart Month* Teach students ways to care for their hearts, such as not smoking, eating healthy, exercising, etc. Give each student a construction paper heart. Have him write and illustrate one way to "love" his heart. Display the hearts on a bulletin board titled *Be Kind to Your Heart*.

27 *No Brainer Day* Give students an easy puzzle or question. Reward them for the correct answer.

28 *Floral Design Day* Make paper flowers with the class. Provide crayons, markers, glitter, paint, different colors of paper, etc. Encourage students to create unusual designs on their flowers. Collect the flowers and create an unusual classroom bouquet.

29 *Leap Year* Brainstorm a list of special activities to complete on this day, such as playing Leap Frog.

5

Sunday	Monday	Tuesday	Wednesday	Thursday	Friday	Saturday

February

FRIENDS FOREVER

LOVE

FOR YOU

PAL

February Gazette

Teacher _____ Date _____

IN THE NEWS

WHAT'S COMING UP

TAKE NOTE

KID'S CORNER

1. areth _____
2. netlvanei _____
3. nfirde _____
4. aydcn _____
5. etews _____

Answers:
1. heart 2. valentine
3. friend 4. candy
5. sweet

Celebrate February!

Dear Family Members,
Here are a few quick-and-easy activities to help you and your child celebrate special days throughout the month of February.

February 8-14 is *Random Acts of Kindness Week*
- With your child, create a list of simple favors and nice things you can do for friends and for other family members. Surprise a different person every day by doing something thoughtful for them, such as leaving small treats and notes or finishing household chores.

On February 18, 1830, the planet *Pluto was discovered* by Clyde Tombaugh
- Venture outside and take a good look at the nighttime sky with your child. Play a game of trying to distinguish planets from stars. Explain to your child that stars appear to twinkle, while planets do not.

February is *National Wild Bird Feeding Month*
- Make homemade bird feeders using peanut butter, bread, and birdseed. Cut slices of day-old bread into various shapes using cookie cutters. Use a drinking straw to make a hole in the top of each shape. Spread a layer of peanut butter on each shape and sprinkle with birdseed. Thread lengths of string through the holes and hang the bird feeders from tree branches.

February is *National Cherry Month*
- Enjoy a tasty cherry pie!
  - 2 8"- or 9"- frozen pie crusts
  - 6 cups of washed, stemmed, and pitted Bing cherries
  - 1¼ cups sugar
  - 3 tablespoons flour
  - 4 tablespoons of instant tapioca

Bake one pie crust according to the package directions. Place prepared cherries in a large bowl and let sit for approximately 15 minutes. Drain excess juice from the bowl. Stir sugar, flour, and tapioca into the cherries. Pour the mixture into the baked pie crust. Cut lattice strips from the second pie crust and place on top of the filling. Bake at 400° for approximately 45 minutes or until the crust is brown.

February is *National Library Lovers' Month*
- Take your child to the library and help him or her obtain a library card. Then, help your child choose books to check out and read. Talk to library employees to find out what other special services and programs the library offers to the public. Many are free!

February is *American Heart Month*
- Exercise by taking a brisk walk with your child, then share a heart healthy snack such as carrot sticks or apple slices. Talk about the importance of a healthy heart.

Read In February!

Dear Family Members,
Here are some books to share with your child to enhance the enjoyment of reading in February.

Abraham Lincoln by Ingri D'Aulaire
- *Vivid illustrations tell the story of Abraham Lincoln's life, from his boyhood in the wilderness to his career as President of the United States.*
- Help your child start a penny collection. Find the oldest penny and the newest penny in your collection. Add a wheat penny to the collection and compare it to a modern coin.

George Washington: A Picture Book Biography by James Cross Giblin
- *This biography offers highlights of the first president's home and family life as well as his leadership and service.*
- Write a letter to the president with your child. Mail the letter to: The President c/o the Office of Presidential Student Correspondence, 1600 Pennsylvania Avenue, Washington, D.C. 20500.

One Zillion Valentines by Frank Modell
- *Marvin and Melvin make special valentines to send in hopes of getting some in return.*
- Provide white , pink, and red construction paper, scissors, and markers for your child to use to make valentines. Mail or deliver the valentines to family members and special friends.

Bee My Valentine by Miriam Cohen
- *A first grade class exchanges valentines with funny results.*
- After reading the story, think of funny valentine puns like those in the story. Cut out heart shapes from paper and have your child write valentine puns on the hearts.

The Coming of Night by James Riordan
- *This folktale from West Africa explains how nighttime animals and sounds came into being.*
- Read this story with your child at bedtime. Listen for nighttime sounds and talk about what animals are active at night.

Bringing the Rain to Kapiti Plain by Verna Aardema
- *A herdsman on the African plain waits patiently for a much-needed rainstorm. Eventually he finds a clever way to pierce a rain cloud and bring relief to the thirsty animals.*
- Have your child look for and name the different African animals in the story. Have him or her draw a picture of a favorite animal from the story.

Aunt Harriet's Underground Railroad in the Sky by Faith Ringgold
- *Cassie and her brother fly into the sky and board a train filled with people escaping to freedom on the Underground Railroad. Harriet Tubman guides the children's journey.*
- Let your child use paint and fabric scraps to create a picture that tells a story. Encourage your child to explain the completed story to you.

A sweet treat for a job well done!

Name _____

Signed _____

Date _____

For _____

WOW

GREAT JOB

NICE WORK

Signed _____

Date _____

LOST A TOOTH!

_____
name

Signed _____

Date _____

A Caring Heart!

_____ has

FRIEND

Signed _____

Date _____

FEBRUARY Writing Activities

February is a great time for appreciating the past, reflecting on the present, and working toward the future. Use writing to help students realize these goals.

Word Bank Words

shadow   envelope
weather   stamp
burrow   Washington
card   Lincoln
valentine   president
heart   candy
groundhog

Choral Reading

Give students a voice in their own education. Have students choose a seasonal poem to read together as a class. Vary the activity by having some lines read by one or several students, or by alternating groups of students. Have the class select important passages and let different students read the lines aloud, emphasizing different words and phrases each time. Discuss the way pace, tone, and volume affect the line readings.

Tasty Treats

Show students how sweet descriptive writing can be! Provide candy labels for students to read. Point out the descriptive words often used to talk about the taste and texture of candy. Give each student a piece of candy to enjoy as they write descriptions about its flavor and texture.

The Life of a Superhero

Have students imagine what life would be like if they could be superheroes. Instruct them to write about what special powers they would have and how they would help others. Let students draw themselves wearing special costumes and write descriptions of how they might look.

Student Spelling Sentences

Motivate students to write creative and interesting sentences for their spelling words using this idea. Collect the sentences students write for a spelling list and choose the most original ones to read aloud during the weekly spelling test. Award extra points to the students who have sentences chosen.

My heart smiled when I saw the valentine.

Strengths, Suggestions, Questions

Help peer editors stay focused and provide writers with useful information using this technique. When reviewing a classmate's work, have the editor fold a piece of paper into three columns labeled *Strengths*, *Suggestions*, and *Questions*. Have editors write at least one thing in each column, then pass the sheet back to the writer with the draft.

Strengths	Suggestions	Questions
It was a very interesting story.	Please add more details to the story.	What happened after the end of the story?
There was a lot of humor in the story.	Clarify who the characters were.	How did the mother react?

A Web Page of Your Own

Challenge students to imagine, design, and write about their own web site. Have students consider what information and graphics they would like to include, and what other web sites they would want to link to their personal site.

Character Letters

Use this activity to combine character analysis and letter writing practice. Allow students to choose a character from a favorite story and write a letter to the character. Have students write questions about the character's actions and behavior, and give the character advice.

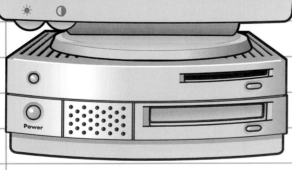

Dear Huck Finn,
You are so imaginative and brave. What is your favorite adventure? How do you always manage to escape? When you grow up, you should go into politics.

Your Friend,
Hank

Story Cubes

Teach students how to "shape" a personal narrative with this great exercise. Have each student cut out a simple six-sided cube pattern. Number the sections 1-6. In the first section, have students write the introduction to a personal narrative. In sections two, three, and four, have them write events from the story. In section five, write the climax to the story. In the last section, write the story ending. Let students fold the pattern to form a cube and secure the sides with tape. To read the story, start in section one and read each side in order.

Bulletin Board Ideas

Give your students "heads up" about groundhogs with this interactive display. Cover the top of the board with blue paper and the bottom with green paper fringed to resemble grass. Add a yellow and orange paper sun in a corner. Copy the large groundhog pattern (page 23) on brown paper and give one to each child to cut out. Have students research and write facts about groundhogs on the patterns. Use a craft knife to cut horizontal slits in the green paper, slightly wider than the patterns. Slide the groundhog patterns into the slits. Let students pull up the patterns and read the facts. This display supports the *Groundhog Greetings* chapter (pages 20-23).

Familiarize students with the achievements of African-Americans. Cover the board with squares of blue, purple, yellow, and orange paper, and a central oval containing the week's topic. Choose a different group of African-Americans each week (for example, scientists, athletes, entertainers, and world leaders). Have students research selected individuals and then write their findings beside a portrait of the featured individual. Use this display to highlight the *Celebrate African-American History* chapter (pages 24-31).

14

STORIES FROM AFRICA

Focus students' attention on books and stories from Africa. Cover the board with orange paper and place a large outline of Africa in the center. Have students cut out red, yellow, black, and green shapes to create a colorful border. As students read African stories and folktales, have them illustrate book covers and display them around the continent shape to encourage others to read the books. Use this bulletin board to complement the *Folktales from Africa* chapter (pages 32-35).

This display is sure to inspire smiles! First, cover the board with red paper. Then, have each student draw a portrait of herself smiling. Post the portraits on the board and accent them with copies of the toothbrush pattern (page 41). Under each portrait, let students write things they can do to keep their teeth healthy. Have students cut out tooth shapes and create a border for the bulletin board. Use this display with the *Smile…It's Dental Health Month!* chapter (pages 36-42).

Students will journey to new frontiers of understanding with this informative bulletin board. Cover the top of the board with blue paper and the bottom with light brown paper. Cut a "trail" the length of the board from dark brown or black paper and post it on the board. Display a map showing the path of the Oregon Trail. Add cottonball clouds to the sky. Give each student an enlarged copy of the covered wagon pattern (page 50) to cut out. Have students write facts about pioneers and the Oregon Trail on the patterns and place them on the trail. Attach paper student-made horses and oxen to the wagons with yarn. Use this display in conjunction with the *Pioneer Trails* chapter (pages 43-52).

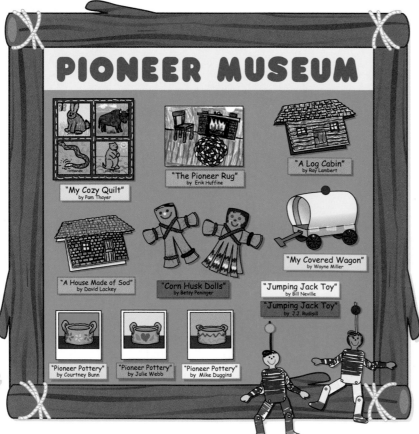

Create a special museum where students can display the crafts they make during the *Pioneer Trails* chapter (pages 43-52). Cover a bulletin board with green paper. Create a border by cutting log shapes from brown paper and accenting them with yarn or string. Post student-made quilts, jumping jack dolls, cornhusk dolls, pioneer diaries, braided rugs, and photographs of pioneer pottery projects on the bulletin board. Add students' names and informative labels, with the title *Pioneer Museum*.

HAVE A HEART!

Reward students with treats from the heart. Cover a bulletin board with blue paper and place a cupid pattern (page 68) on the board. Let students cut out paper hearts and decorate them with glitter, beads, ribbons, etc. On the back of each heart, write a reward or attach a treat. Post the hearts on the board. Reward students by letting them choose a heart and enjoy the treat on the back. Accent the *Be My Valentine!* chapter (pages 57-68) with this sweet bulletin board.

Students will love making their marks on these handmade hearts, which you can use to accent student work. Cover the bulletin board with pink paper. Have students cut large heart shapes from white paper, write their names on the hearts, and then personalize them with thumbprint designs in a variety of colored, washable inks. Let students cut out the heart shapes. Post them on the board with students' best work, including activities from the *Be My Valentine!* chapter (pages 57-68).

Mrs. Gromley's Class
Room 204
Carson Elementary School
Greensboro, NC 27408

SPECIAL DELIVERY

33¢

I have a dream

FEBRUARY

TO:
John
Thank you for letting me play with your soccer ball. Luke

WENDY Luke Amanda Lynn

Caroline Trey Cole Ray Kenya Ethan Tyrone

Amy Adam Jacob COURTNEY Leslie Jerry

Kim
Hi Kim, I liked eating lunch with you. Kenya

Encourage students to send kind messages to classmates with this display. Cover the board with yellow paper. Write your class address in the top left corner. Have students create a large postage stamp depicting February events and place it in the top right corner with the postmark *Special Delivery*. Give each child a sheet of paper. Have students fold their papers in half, write their names on the fronts, then place them in the "To:" section of the bulletin board. Encourage students to write friendly greetings, letters, and thank you notes to classmates, who can lift the flaps to read their messages. This bulletin board supports the *Be My Valentine!* (pages 57-68) and *The Post Office* (pages 74-78) chapters.

HEALTHY HEARTS ARE HAPPY HEARTS

Kevin

Avoiding stress

Doing drugs

Riley

Heather

Smoking cigarettes

Swimming

Sally

Todd

Eating low-fat foods

Eating cereal

Julie

Playing sports

Eating vegetables

Amanda

Relaxing

Going to the doctor

Patrick

Students will put their hearts into their work with this informative display. Cover the board with blue paper. Post sentence strips on the board listing activities that are good or bad for the heart, along with an envelope containing smiling and frowning paper hearts. Ask students to match smiling hearts to healthy habits and frowning hearts to unhealthy habits. Decorate the board by having students draw pictures of themselves doing things that are good for their hearts. Post the drawings, and refer to this bulletin board during your study of the *Heart Smart* chapter (pages 69-73).

18

Give your students a chance to change the world by having them write what they would do as president. Cover the board with red, white, and blue paper. Give students copies of the hat patterns (page 86) to cut out. Have each child draw and color a self-portrait and attach it to her hat. Let students draw and cut out speech balloons and write presidential proclamations on them. Use this bulletin board display to accentuate the *Presidents' Day* chapter (pages 79-86).

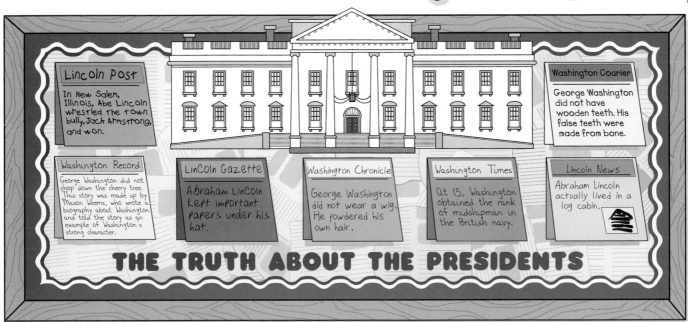

Help your students get the scoop on George Washington and Abraham Lincoln with this display. Cover the board with newspaper. Enlarge and cut out the White House pattern (page 85), color the windows and doors, and place it in the top center portion of the board. Have each student fold a sheet of paper and illustrate it to resemble a newspaper with a title and headline. Next, have students research myths and facts about Washington and Lincoln. Let them write the information on their "newspapers" and post them on the board for other students to read. This display supports the *Presidents' Day* chapter (pages 79-86).

Groundhog Greetings!

The forecast calls for fun, fun, fun with these Groundhog Day activities! Every February 2, the groundhog predicts the next six weeks' weather. Legend says that if it sees its shadow, more wintry weather is on the way; if not, spring is just around the corner!

Did You Know?

- German immigrants to Punxsutawney, Pennsylvania, have celebrated Groundhog Day since 1887. Tradition holds that if the groundhog sees its shadow there will be six more weeks of winter.
- On February 2, "Punxsutawney Phil" emerges from his burrow, looks for his shadow, then makes his prediction.
- Canada's weather forecasting groundhog is known as "Wiarton Willie."
- February 2 is also St. Brigid's Day, or Candlemas. This traditional rhyme may explain the origins of Groundhog Day: "If Candlemas Day be bright and clear, there'll be two winters in the year."

Literature Selections

Gretchen Groundhog, It's Your Day! by Abby Levine: Whitman, Albert & Company, 1998. (Picture book, 32 pg.) Gretchen is left with the burden of predicting the weather, because her Great-Uncle Gus is too old to look for his shadow.
It's Groundhog Day! by Steven Kroll: Scholastic, Inc., 1991. (Picture book, 32 pg.) Roland Raccoon is determined to stop Godfrey Groundhog from looking for his shadow.
Geoffrey Groundhog Predicts the Weather by Bruce Koscielniak: Houghton Mifflin Co., 1995. (Picture book, 32 pg.) Geoffrey Groundhog becomes a celebrity after accurately predicting the weather, but can he handle it?

Spring or Winter?

Early spring or long winter? Use this student-made mural to display the groundhog's prediction. Have students work together to create a mural of a groundhog's habitat. Provide butcher paper, markers, crayons, and construction paper, and have students decorate a mural that includes trees, rocks, underground tunnels, and burrows. Give each student a copy of the small groundhog pattern (page 23) to color and personalize. Let students write their predictions on the backs of the patterns. On Groundhog Day, attach the groundhogs to the mural. Leave space at the top of the mural to record whether or not the groundhog saw his shadow. Extend the activity by tracking daily temperatures for several weeks. Choose one student each day to write the date and color in the temperature on a thermometer pattern (page 23). Have the student place the thermometer beside his groundhog on the mural. Continue until each student has had a turn. Was the groundhog's prediction accurate?

Not Just Groundhogs

Groundhogs are not the only weather predictors—wooly worms, sheep, cows, hornets, and turkeys are also known for their forecasting skills. Weather folklore says that if sheep gather close together, or if cows lie in a field, then rain is on the way. If a turkey's feathers are thick at Thanksgiving, or if hornets build their nests close to the ground, then a harsh winter is ahead. Create a class book of weather folklore using *The Farmer's Almanac* and reference books. Let students research weather folklore, write an example, and illustrate it. Ask students to share their findings with the class.

If the wooly bear caterpillar has a wide brown band, then winter will be mild.

If it has a thin band, then winter will be harsh.

If Groundhog Day is bright and clear,
Winter will be staying here.
If Groundhog Day is cold and gray,
Sunny Spring is on the way!

by: David L.

Groundhog Day Cards

Have students make cards with peek-a-boo groundhogs. Give each student 2 sheets of construction paper. Carefully cut a 3 1/2" long horizontal slit in the upper portion of one sheet. Under the slit, have students write their own Groundhog Day sayings, rhymes, and predictions. Next, give each child a small groundhog pattern (page 23) to color and cut out. Glue the pattern to a 7 1/2" strip of cardboard. Tape the sheets of construction paper together, leaving space at the bottom for the handle to extend below the edge of the card. Use the handle to position the groundhog between the sheets of construction paper. Let students push their groundhogs up through the slits in the cards and predict the weather. If desired, post the Groundhog Day cards around the *Spring or Winter?* mural (page 20).

You Be the Groundhog

Let students be groundhogs for a day! Explain that if the groundhog sees its shadow, it gets scared and rushes back into its burrow. This means there will be six more weeks of winter weather. If the groundhog does not see its shadow, however, spring is just around the corner. Bring in a large cardboard box and cut a hole in each end. Provide paint, markers, construction paper, glue, fabric scraps, etc., and let students decorate the box like a groundhog's home by painting trees, flowers, grass, snow, etc. Next, let each student crawl through the tunnel pretending to be a groundhog peeping out of its hole. Have the "groundhog" tell the class whether or not he sees his shadow. Finally, use large or small groundhog patterns (page 23) to make a pictograph detailing students' predictions.

Shadow Books

These groundhogs will be seeing their shadows more than once! Give each student a copy of the large groundhog pattern (page 23). Have students color the pattern brown to represent the groundhog and then trace the pattern several times on black construction paper to represent its shadow. Have students cut out the traced patterns. Provide several reference books and challenge students to write one fact about groundhogs on each shadow page, such as *Groundhogs are also known as woodchucks*, with a white pencil. Fasten the groundhog patterns with a brad at bottom left, putting the brown pattern on top. Fan the shadows out one at a time to reveal the groundhog facts. Display the completed books at a reading center where students can learn about groundhogs.

The groundhog is also called the woodchuck.

The groundhog is a member of the squirrel family.

Groundhogs have 22 teeth.

How Tall is Your Shadow?

It depends upon the time of day! Have students work in pairs. On a sunny day, let students go outside several times to measure their shadows. Have students use chalk to label, name, and mark the beginning and end points of each of their shadows. Use the same spot each time so students will have a visual comparison of how their shadows change throughout the day. At the end of the day, talk about the results with the class. Allow students to make observations and ask questions. When are shadows the longest? The shortest? Why?

I'm Your Shadow

Students will be seeing double with this shadow game! Take students outside on a sunny day and let them work in pairs to be each others' shadows. Choose one student in each pair to be the shadow. Have each pair of students face each other. One student will move and the "shadow" must mimic her movements. Let students switch roles so everyone has a turn being a shadow.

Shadow Pie

Conclude your class celebration of Groundhog Day with a tasty treat! Prepare one box of instant chocolate pudding. Spread the pudding on an 8" pie crust. Make a groundhog stencil by cutting out the large groundhog pattern (page 23) from the center of a piece of paper. Place the stencil on top of the pudding. Crush vanilla cookies and sprinkle around the edges of the stencil. Remove the stencil to reveal the groundhog's shadow! Serve the shadow pie to students and read the book *It's Groundhog Day!* by Steven Kroll while students eat their treats.

large groundhog

COPY and CUT

small groundhog

°F		°C
100		
90		
80		
70		
60		40
50		30
40		20
30		10
20		0
10		10
0		20
-10		

thermometer

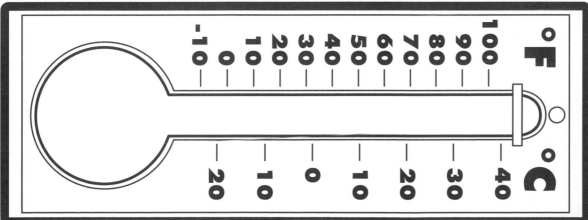

Celebrate African-American History

African-American History Month was established in 1926 as Negro History Week. The commemoration took place in February because the birthdays of Frederick Douglass (1817 or 1818) and Abraham Lincoln (February 12, 1809), both instrumental in the abolition of slavery, fall in February. Expanded in duration and scope, African-American History Month provides an opportunity to examine the contributions of African-Americans, to remind all Americans of their roots, and to promote mutual respect among races.

○ **Douglass and Lincoln** ○

Did You Know?

★ African-American inventor Garrett A. Morgan designed the gas mask in 1912. He went on to invent the traffic light in 1923.

★ In 1905 Madame C.J. Walker marketed hair care products for women and became the first African-American millionaire businesswoman.

★ The phrase, "the real McCoy" was coined by customers wanting to buy an original lubricating machine invented in 1873 by Elijah McCoy, an African-American.

Literature Selections

Take a Walk in Their Shoes by Glennette Tilley Turner: Penguin, 1992. (Biography, 174 pg.) Contains biographies of 14 outstanding African-Americans, as well as skits which provide insight into each individual's life.

I See the Rhythm by Toyomi Igus: Childrens Book Press, 1998. (Poetry book, 32 pg.) The history of African-American music, told in poems and presented with colorful paintings.

Gifts of Our People by Portia George: Judson Press, 1995. (Nonfiction book, 40 pg.) An alphabet book of African-American history.

Who Am I?

Help students learn about the African-Americans who helped shape the United States. List notable African-Americans and assign one to each student (or group) to research. Next, have each child present her research as if she were the person, without revealing that person's name. Challenge students to identify each historical figure by asking questions such as, *Are you a scientist?* or *Did you live during the Civil War?* Create lists of questions, answers, and/or clues to help students identify each individual.

Benjamin Banneker (1731-1806)

Benjamin Banneker is recognized for his contributions to the world of science. He grew up on his family's farm and was taught to read by his grandmother. Once, fascinated by the inner workings of a watch, he carved wooden replicas of the watch's parts and made his own wooden clock, which worked accurately for more than 40 years! Banneker taught himself astronomy and mathematics, and was hired to help plan the layout of the United States' new capital, Washington, D.C. Banneker also published an almanac containing astronomical observations and weather predictions. The almanac so impressed Thomas Jefferson and others that it was used by opponents of slavery to argue the intelligence and skill of African-Americans.

Honor Benjamin Banneker for his part in planning the United States capital. Let students use a variety of craft materials and art supplies to construct model memorials to Benjamin Banneker. Ask them to write paragraphs explaining why and where the memorial should be built, then let them share their models and paragraphs with the class.

Harriet Tubman (1821-1913)

Harriet Tubman was a slave in Maryland until she was 30 years old, when she escaped along the Underground Railroad, a network of people who helped slaves escape to freedom. Tubman joined the Underground Railroad as a "conductor," making many dangerous trips south, and helping free over 300 slaves. She was never caught and never lost a passenger. Harriet Tubman continued to help others by serving as a scout and nurse during the Civil War, by being active in the women's rights movement, and by building a home for elderly and needy African-Americans.

Harriet Tubman dedicated her life to helping others. Ask students to think about ways they can help others in their daily lives. Allow each student to make a construction paper train car from a rectangle and two small circles. Have each student write on his train car one way he can help others. Punch a hole in the front and back of each car and connect with yarn. Draw a railroad track on a bulletin board and display the connected train cars on the track with the title *Harriet Tubman's Helping Railroad*.

Scott Joplin (1868-1917)

Carter C. Woodson (1875-1950)

Scott Joplin, the son of former slaves, was one of the first American composers, writing rags, marches, and an opera. As a child he studied classical piano, then left home as a young man to play piano and travel. He settled in Missouri to compose ragtime music. Ragtime, short for "ragged time," was an early form of jazz. Joplin was not recognized as an important composer until after his death, when the movie, *The Sting*, revived interest in his music. He was posthumously awarded a Pulitzer Prize for music in 1976.

Listen to Scott Joplin's most famous composition, *Maple Leaf Rag*, named for a saloon where he played. Let each child cut a maple leaf shape from construction paper. Listen to the song again and have each student draw a picture on her leaf based on the images the music brings to mind. Next, let students share their drawings and discuss how the music makes them feel. Display the maple leaves on a board around the title *Scott Joplin's "Maple Leaf Rag."*

Carter G. Woodson was a historian and the founder of African-American History Month. Self-taught during his early years, Woodson worked as a coal miner and school teacher to pay for his education. He earned his Ph.D. from Harvard University and started the Association for the Study of Negro Life and History. The association was established to educate African-Americans about the contributions and achievements of their ancestors, and to promote the study of African-American history in school curriculums.

Carter Woodson hoped that all Americans would share an interest and pride in each other's roots and gain a mutual respect for all races and cultural backgrounds. Have students study their ancestors, learn about the countries they are from, and what contributions people from those countries have made to the world. Have each child share his heritage with the class.

Marian Anderson (1897-1993)

Langston Hughes (1902-1967)

Marian Anderson was the first African-American to join the Metropolitan Opera in New York City, paving the way for other African-American singers. As a child, she sang in her church choir and tried to attend a music school, but was turned away because she was African-American. After private lessons, she won first prize at a New York Philharmonic voice competition. When the Daughters of the American Revolution kept her from performing in their building because she was African-American, Eleanor Roosevelt resigned from the group and arranged for Anderson to sing in front of 75,000 people at the Lincoln Memorial. Marian Anderson received many awards including the Presidential Medal of Freedom and a Grammy Lifetime Achievement Award.

Introduce students to opera. Play a recording of opera music and have students listen for a story in the music. Explain that even though opera is often sung in a different language, the music and style of singing help the audience understand the story. Have students write a short story based upon their interpretation of the opera. Next, tell students the actual plot of the opera, then compare the two stories.

Langston Hughes started writing poetry as a boy and grew to be one of America's most important poets. He lived in Harlem, a neighborhood in New York City, frequenting blues and jazz clubs and writing poetry inspired by the music. Hughes wrote plays, novels, essays, editorials, and poetry about the African-American experience and conditions at the time. During the 1920s, Harlem was the center of African-American creativity. This period, called the Harlem Renaissance, produced many important African-American writers, musicians, dancers, artists, and intellectuals.

Langston Hughes also wrote poetry for children. Let students read Hughes' poems in the alphabet book, *The Sweet and Sour Animal Book* (Oxford University Press, Inc., 1997). Assign a letter of the alphabet to each child and have him write an imaginative animal poem using the letter. Compile the poems into a class alphabet poetry book.

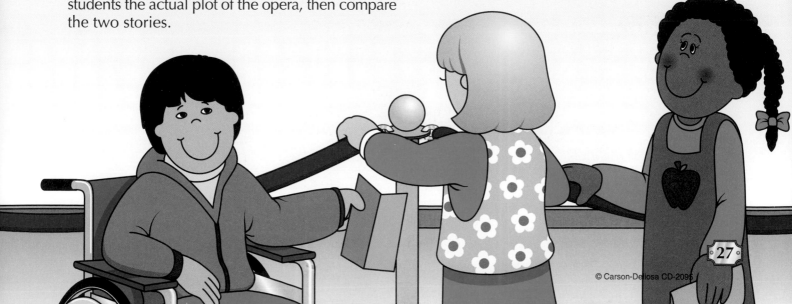

◦Thurgood Marshall (1908-1993)◦

Thurgood Marshall was the first African-American appointed to the Supreme Court. Before his twenty-year service as a Supreme Court Justice, Marshall was a lawyer for the NAACP (National Association for the Advancement of Colored People). He worked to end segregation and helped African-Americans fight for civil rights. Marshall won a landmark case, *Brown v. the Board of Education*, overturning the "separate but equal" policy that allowed school segregation. Marshall argued that separate was not equal, saying, "Equal means getting the same thing, at the same time and in the same place."

In the spirit of Thurgood Marshall, set up a conflict resolution court to help students settle disputes. Select several students to serve on the class supreme court. Instruct them to listen to both sides of arguments and make decisions about how to resolve the problems. Set aside a certain time each day or week when "cases" will be heard. Rotate judges periodically to allow each child a chance to be mediator.

◦ Jackie Robinson (1919-1972) ◦

Jackie Robinson excelled in sports, and wanted to be a professional athlete. During his time, however, sports were segregated, so Robinson played in the Negro League. The Brooklyn Dodgers realized his excellence, and he became the first African-American to play Major League Baseball. He faced discrimination from fans and other players, but felt that persevering was important for the future of African-American athletes. Robinson was named National League Rookie of the Year and Most Valuable Player, and was inducted into the Baseball Hall of Fame. Robinson became a businessman and politician, working to improve the lives of African-Americans.

Talk with students about character traits Jackie Robinson demonstrated by staying in Major League Baseball. Let students create baseball cards on index cards. Have them draw pictures of Robinson on the fronts of the cards, and on the backs list character traits he displayed, such as courage, perseverance, and patience. Let students trade and compare cards.

n-Dellosa CD-2095

Faith Ringgold (1930-)

Faith Ringgold is an artist and children's book writer. She grew up in Harlem among African-American role models such as Thurgood Marshall, Mary McLeod Bethune, and Duke Ellington. Ringgold's art has been shown in museums around the world. She is best known for her painted story quilts, which combine acrylic painting on canvas and quilted fabric. Faith Ringgold has written numerous children's books, including stories that accompany her quilts, and stories about famous African-Americans such as Dr. Martin Luther King, Jr., Rosa Parks, and Harriet Tubman.

Ringgold's first book, *Tar Beach*, won a Caldecott Honor and the Coretta Scott King Award for Illustration. Let students look at *Tar Beach* and other books by Ringgold, including *Aunt Harriet's Underground Railroad in the Sky*, *Dancing at the Louvre*, and *Dinner at Aunt Connie's House*. Let students use a technique similar to Ringgold's to create their own story quilts. On a square of paper, have each student paint a picture that tells a story, then glue the paintings to larger sheets of paper. Below the painting, have each student write a short story about her illustration. Let students finish their story quilts by gluing fabric scraps around the borders of their paintings.

General Colin Powell (1937-)

General Colin Powell rose through the ranks to become a four-star general and Chairman of the Joint Chiefs of Staff. He joined the Army in college and served in Vietnam, earning a Purple Heart for his service. Powell held various high-level positions before being appointed National Security Advisor. This led to his appointment as Chairman of the Joint Chiefs of Staff, making him the youngest officer and first African-American to hold this post. Now retired, General Powell is actively involved with several nonprofit organizations, such as the United Negro College Fund and The Boys and Girls Clubs of America.

General Powell is an outstanding leader and has been awarded many medals of honor including the Distinguished Service Medal, the Bronze Star, the Purple Heart, the Presidential Medal of Freedom, and the Congressional Gold Medal. Divide the class into small groups and ask each group to research one of these medals. Have them make a model of the medal and write a short paragraph telling why it is awarded. Display the medals and paragraphs around a picture of General Powell.

One day I went to the park with my dog Cody. We played fetch and had fun. Cody licked me in the face and it was funny! by: Faith

General Powell's Medals

Ringgold's Story Quilts

29

Oprah Winfrey (1954-)

Oprah Winfrey is a businesswoman, philanthropist, and advocate for many social causes. At 19, Winfrey was the youngest person and first African-American woman to anchor a news show on Nashville, Tennessee television. She became the host of a Chicago morning show that was so successful its name was changed to *The Oprah Winfrey Show*. She shifted the focus of her show to emphasize helping others, began raising money to fund college scholarships, and created a book club that promotes literature, reading, and lifelong learning.

Talk with students about how Oprah's book club has renewed interest in reading. Get students excited about reading by starting your own book club. Like Oprah, choose a book, then provide as many copies as possible to the class. Once every student has read the book, host a book chat complete with snacks. Before the book chat, have students prepare questions and statements about the book. During the chat, make sure each child has a chance to talk. Finally, create a Top Ten Class Favorite Books list to display in your classroom.

Mae Jemison (1956-)

Mae Jemison is a medical doctor, scientist, and former astronaut. As a child she was interested in science and started college when she was 16. Jemison served as a Peace Corps Medical Officer in West Africa and works to improve medical care in other countries. She was selected by NASA to be an astronaut and became the first African-American woman in space. As Science Mission Specialist, she conducted experiments aboard the space shuttle Endeavor. Jemison also founded the Jemison Group, Inc., dedicated to using science and technology to help developing countries.

Mae Jemison is dedicated to improving the image of scientists, as well as promoting careers in science. Before sharing information about Mae Jemison, ask students to draw a picture of a scientist. Compare and contrast their drawings to see different images of scientists. Help students understand that a scientist does not have to look like Albert Einstein, but can look like Mae Jemison, or even themselves!

African-American History Crossword Puzzle

Name _____

Use the clues and the word bank at right to solve the crossword puzzle. If you need help, look up more information about each person in the word list to help you solve the puzzle.

Word Bank

Attucks

Bethune

Drew

Ellington

Haley

Henson

Parks

Rudolph

Terrell

Truth

Across

4. Sojourner _____ was a former slave who traveled around telling people the truth about slavery.
5. Matthew _____ was an adventurer, and the first person to reach the North Pole.
6. Duke _____ was a world famous jazz composer and musician.
8. Wilma _____ overcame polio to become the first American woman to win three gold medals in a single Olympic Games.

Down

1. Rosa _____ refused to give up her seat on the bus to a white person, as was the law at the time.
2. Mary McLeod _____ founded a hospital to treat African-Americans and train African-American doctors and nurses, when other hospitals refused.
3. Crispus _____ was the first patriot to lose his life in the Revolutionary War, during the Boston Massacre.
5. Alex _____ was the first African-American writer to win the Pulitzer Prize, for his novel *Roots*.
7. Mary Church _____ was one of the founders of the NAACP (National Association for the Advancement of Colored People).
9. Charles ____ discovered a way to preserve blood, and served as director of the first U.S. Red Cross blood bank.

Folktales from Africa

Inspire students to explore Africa's rich oral tradition. Characterized by larger-than-life personalities and fantastic storylines, these tales relate the universal theme of overcoming adversity through individual action. Many attempt to explain natural phenomena, such as why the sky is blue or why birds live in trees. Use these African folktales as inspiration for imaginative student writing, reading, art, and craft activities.

The Flying Tortoise: An Igbo Tale

Retold by Tololwa M. Mollel (Clarion Books, 1994). 32 pages

A greedy tortoise tricks a flock of birds into letting him fly with them to Skyland, where he repays them by stealing their feast of exotic foods. When his wings are taken away, the tortoise has no easy way to return to land. His crash-landing explains why tortoises have checkered shells.

Use this activity to talk about character. Although Mbeku the tortoise was selfish and greedy, he was also smart, resourceful, and clever. Have students brainstorm positive and negative character traits, then explore the meanings of the traits. Illustrate the qualities by having students draw and cut out turtle shapes, then cut and glue paper to the turtle shapes to create a checkered shell. On each piece of shell, have students write a character trait Mbeku exhibited. Cut a sheet of paper so it fits underneath the turtle shape. Have students use the sheet to describe Mbeku and the events of the story using the character words written on the shell fragments.

The Coming of Night: A Yoruba Tale from West Africa

by James Riordan (Millbrook Press, 1999). 32 pages

Aje, the daughter of the river goddess Yemoya, leaves her underwater home to live in the Land of the Shining Day. Here, the sun shines all the time and Aje begins to miss the cool darkness of her former home. To comfort Aje, her husband sends messengers to bring the peaceful nighttime from the river to the land.

Night is like the cool shade of a tree over a sunny beach.

In the story, Aje misses the sounds and feelings that night brings. Aje tells her husband, "Night is a cool veil that curtains the day's warm bed. It is the welcome rest that refreshes a weary soul." Ask students to write poetic descriptions of night on black paper with white or yellow crayons. Have them draw and cut out moths, owls, bats, leopards, and other night animals. Glue them to the paper to illustrate the things night brings.

A Story, A Story

Retold by Gail E. Haley (Atheneum, 1970). 36 pages **Caldecott Medal Winner**

Anase, the Spider Man, seeks a golden box of stories from the Sky God. In return for the stories, Anase must obtain three earthly things for the Sky God. When Anase finally brings the story box to Earth, he opens it and scatters the stories all around the world.

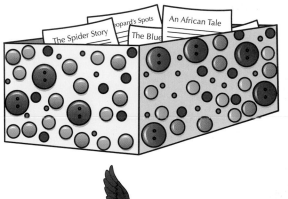

In African folklore, many stories feature clever characters that outwit others and overcome great obstacles. The "Spider story" is part of this popular genre. Decorate a shoe box to use as a story holder for imaginative student writing. Cover the box with colorful paper, then add sequins, glitter, buttons, etc. Have students write their own folktales explaining how something came to be, such as how the zebra got its stripes, how the leopard got its spots, or why the sky is blue. Place the completed folktales in the story box. Have students take turns selecting stories from the box and reading them aloud.

The Hatseller and the Monkeys

by Baba Wagué Diakité (Scholastic Press, 1999). 32 pages

A hatseller sets out to sell his wares. After he stops to rest under a tree, he awakes to find his hats stolen by mischievous monkeys. Quite by accident, the hatseller tricks the monkeys into giving back his hats.

After sharing this story with the class, read a Russian version of this folktale, *Caps for Sale* by Esphyr Slobodkina (Scholastic Inc., 1940. Storybook, 48 pages). Have students compare the stories. Create a version of a Venn diagram by providing three hats—one labeled *The Hatseller and the Monkeys*, one labeled *Caps for Sale*, and another labeled *Both*. Have students write specific details from each story on index cards or strips of paper, and place them in the appropriate hat. Write any similarities between the stories and place them in the hat labeled *Both*. Read the sentences in each hat and discuss how the stories are alike and different.

33

Bringing the Rain to Kapiti Plain

by Verna Aardema (The Dial Press, 1981). 26 pages

Ki-pat and his herd wait patiently for the rain to arrive on the parched, dry Kapiti Plain. A fascinating series of events leads Ki-pat to an idea that finally brings the much needed rain.

Have students compare and contrast the illustrations in the book and talk about droughts and rainstorms. Point out the dry, brown fields of the drought and the lush, green pastures after the rainstorm. Give each student a piece of paper to fold in half. On one side of the paper, have students draw a drought scene on an African plain, and on the other side, the plain after a rainstorm. Have students write words in each scene describing the weather conditions.

Drought — hot parched dry scorched

Rain — cool refreshing wet green

Abiyoyo

by Pete Seeger (Macmillan Publishing Company, 1986). 48 pages

A boy and his father are banished from town for being "different." But when scary Abiyoyo shows up, they use the talents that originally forced them out of town to make Abiyoyo disappear, earning the trust and respect of the townspeople.

Reenact the story of Abiyoyo! Have students sit in a circle, with a volunteer in the middle pretending to be Abiyoyo. Choose another student to be the magician. Give him a special wand made from a long cardboard tube. Play the tape-recorded version of the story. As the children sing the song, have Abiyoyo dance inside the circle. During the song, have the magician tap Abiyoyo and say "Zoop!," making Abiyoyo disappear (to rejoin the circle). The magician then becomes Abiyoyo, passing his wand to another member of the circle, who then becomes the new magician.

Why the Sun and the Moon Live in the Sky

by Elphinstone Dayrell (Scholastic, Inc., 1968.) 32 pages **Caldecott Honor Book**

The sun wants his friend, the water, to visit, so he builds a house that is large enough to hold the water and all its creatures. When the water arrives, he fills the house to overflowing, causing the sun and his wife the moon to rise higher and higher in the sky.

Encourage students to design and draw houses for the water and its animals. Let them draw their pictures with crayons on white construction paper. Add an underwater look to the pictures by having students paint over their drawings with blue watercolor paint. Give the pictures a 3-dimensional effect by gluing shells or sand to them, then display them in your classroom.

Imani in the Belly

by Deborah M. Newton Chocolate (BridgeWater Books, 1994.) 32 pages

Simba, a terrible beast, is swallowing the people and animals of Imani's village. When the beast swallows Imani's family, her courage and faith save the day. Imani makes Simba cough, dispersing the animals in his belly to different locations, where they reside to this day.

Let students draw and color a wild beast like Simba. Near the mouth of the creature, cut a slit using a craft knife. Have students cut out squares of paper slightly smaller than the slit. On each square, let students draw an animal to go inside the creature's belly. Attach a strip of red paper to each square and have students describe where the animal landed and where it now lives. Slide the strips through the opening. Make a pocket by attaching a piece of paper to the back of the drawing to hold the strips. Students can pull the red strips to find out where the animals landed.

35

Smile...
It's Dental Health Month!

Enjoy great grins in your classroom by celebrating National Children's Dental Health Month! This chapter will help students understand the importance of good dental habits. Students will learn about brushing, flossing, the forms and functions of teeth, and the process of tooth decay.

Did You Know?

Children have 20 teeth, while adults have 32. The difference? Adults also have *bicuspids*, teeth with two points, used for crushing food.

The roots of *primary*, or "baby" teeth start to dissolve at about six years old, and eventually fall out.

Enamel, the outer covering of teeth, is the hardest substance in the body—even harder than bone!

Chewing sticks, gnawed and brush-like on one end, and pointed and toothpick-like on the other, were used by Babylonians as early as 3500 BC.

Early toothpaste ingredients included cinnamon, strawberries, and burned bread.

Andrew's Loose Tooth
by Robert Munsch: Scholastic Inc., 1998. (Storybook, 29 pg.) A fantasy about a boy and a tooth that just won't come out.
The Lost Tooth Club by Arden Johnson: Tricycle Press, 1998. (Picture book, 32 pg.) A story about determination, problem solving, and the desire to belong.
The Story of the Tooth Fairy by Tom Paxton: William Morrow & Co., 1996. (Storybook, 32 pg.) An imaginative story touching on themes of trust, cooperation, and friendship.
Throw Your Tooth on the Roof: Tooth Traditions from Around the World by Selby B. Beeler: Houghton Mifflin Co., 1998. (Hardcover, 32 pg.) Features traditions from about 60 countries. Includes a world map and an age-appropriate dental overview.

Make a Dental Health Mobile!

Introduce your study of dental health with these hanging helpers! Give each student copies of the toothbrush, toothpaste, dental floss, and milk carton patterns (page 41) and an enlarged copy of the tooth pattern (pages 42). Have students write *Healthy habits make super smiles!* on the tooth pattern, then color and cut out the patterns. Next, have students punch holes in the patterns and tie them together with string, balancing them so they hang freely. Hang the mobiles from the ceiling or from students' desks.

Healthy Habits Make Super Smiles!

MILK MILK

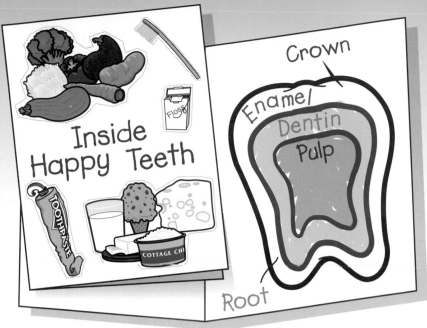

Dental Diagram

Students will get to the "root" of under-standing their teeth with this collage and diagram project. Give each student a copy of the tooth pattern (page 42) on a folded 11" x 17" sheet of paper. Recreate the tooth diagram at left on an overhead transparency, and let students draw and label the different parts of a tooth on the patterns. On the front page of the project, have students write the title *Inside Happy Teeth*. Around the title, have students cut and paste pictures of foods and dental care products which contribute to healthy teeth. Display the projects on a bulletin board titled *Inside Happy Teeth*.

The Plaque Attack

Set up an experiment center that will show students the hazards of too many sugars and sweets. Explain that sugars and acids in some foods dissolve calcium and help create plaque. Plaque is a clear bacterial film that combines with sugars to form acids which eat through tooth enamel, causing tooth decay and gum disease. Explain that eggshells and teeth both contain calcium, then perform this experiment.

Fill clear plastic cups with different liquids, such as water, dark soft drinks, vinegar, tea, coffee, and fruit juices. Label the contents of the cups, then drop a large, clean piece of eggshell into each. Over a two-day period, have students examine the shells for changes in color, texture, hardness, etc. Have students record their findings on copies of the tooth pattern (page 42). (Expect dark liquids to stain the shells. Vinegar and sugary juices will dissolve or discolor the shells.)

Cavity Gravity

Emphasize the seriousness of tooth decay by showing how cavities damage teeth. Poke a hole in an apple with the point of a pencil, representing a cavity in a tooth. Over a two-day period, have students observe changes in the apple's appearance. Encourage students to think about how cavities affect teeth over time, and record their observations on copies of the tooth pattern (page 42).

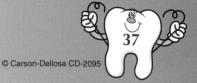

37

Happy, Healthy Teeth

(sing to the tune of *Old MacDonald*)
Teach your students to sing this song during brushing and flossing activities.

Brush your teeth and floss them, too,
For happy, healthy teeth!
Drink your milk and don't eat sweets,
For happy, healthy teeth!
With a brush, brush here, and a floss, floss there,
Here a brush, there a floss, don't forget to rinse, rinse!
See your dentist twice a year
For happy, healthy teeth!

Sing While You Brush

Make craft stick or tongue depressor "toothbrushes." Fringe narrow, tabbed strips of white paper and glue the tabs to the ends of the craft sticks. Follow the instructions for making fingertip tooth puppets (see *Flossing Finger Puppets*, below). Read the *How to Brush* instructions (page 39) to students and teach them the *Happy, Healthy Teeth* song (at left). Let them sing and use their fringed toothbrushes to practice properly brushing the fronts, backs, and sides of the fingertip tooth patterns (page 41).

Brushing Up!

Students will enjoy practicing their brushing skills with this painting activity. For each student, provide an old toothbrush, white paint, and a copy of the tooth pattern (page 42). Have students cut out the tooth pattern and trace it on grey, brown, or yellow construction paper. Have students practice "brushing" their paper teeth with paint and watch them turn white! Finish with a talk about the importance of regular brushing.

Flossing Finger Puppets

Strong flossing skills will be at your students' fingertips with this activity. Reproduce one set of tabbed fingertip tooth patterns (page 41) for each student. Have students cut out the patterns and size them to fit their fingers by overlapping the tabs and taping them so they fit snugly. Pair students, then read aloud the *How to Floss* instructions (page 39). As you read, have students take turns gently flossing their partner's "teeth" with yarn, string, or real dental floss. Teach students the *Happy, Healthy Teeth* song (above). Let them sing and practice proper flossing techniques.

How to Brush

Angle the brush along the gumline. Brush back and forth and up and down, using short strokes. Brush the inner, outer, and biting surfaces of every tooth, using the tip of the brush to reach behind teeth. Remember to brush the tongue and use fluoride mouthwash. Dentists recommend toothbrushes that have small heads and soft bristles, and emphasize—*thoroughness* and *frequency* matter most of all!

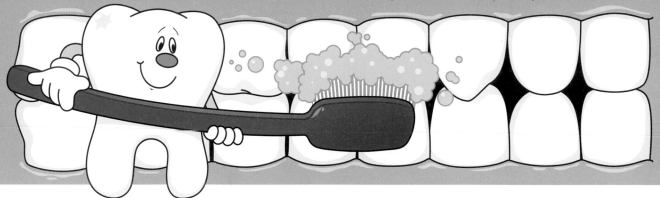

How to Floss

Break off an 18" piece of floss. Wrap most of the floss around the pointer finger of one hand and the rest around the pointer finger of the other hand. Use a gentle, rubbing motion to guide floss between teeth, below the gumline. Form a C-shape along the side of each tooth, then use a gentle up-and-down motion to remove plaque from the gumline and between teeth. Repeat this process for each tooth, using a fresh portion of floss for each tooth by unrolling a new segment from the supply wrapped around the first finger. Remember never to force the floss or snap it into the gums. Minor bleeding may be expected.

FLOSS

For Miles of Smiles

1. Brush twice daily
2. Floss nightly
3. Limit snacks

Smile!

Miles of Smiles Poster

Encourage students to think about dental care by making a healthy teeth poster. Give each student a sheet of colored construction paper and an enlarged tooth pattern (page 42). Use an instant camera to photograph smiling students. Have students cut out and paste their photos to the lower left corner of the construction paper. Cut a circle in the tooth pattern and glue it to the paper so the student's face shows through the circle. As a class, brainstorm healthy dental habits and write them on the tooth patterns. Have students title their posters, *For Miles of Smiles*. Let them take the posters home and hang them as reminders to keep their smiles healthy. If possible, take students to a dentist's office or invite a dentist to visit the class to continue your discussion of dental health.

39

Tooth Totes

What should students do when they lose a tooth? Be prepared! Let students make tooth tote pouches. 1. Give each student an 8½" x 3" felt or construction paper rectangle. 2. Have them fold the bottom 3" upward so it overlaps the central section. 3. Secure the left and right edges with glue. (Tape or staples will work for paper pouches.) After the glue dries, let students use crayons, markers, sequins, glitter, and buttons to decorate the pouches. 4. Instruct students to fold the remaining (top) section of the rectangle down to form a flap. Students can secure the flap with hook-and-loop fasteners, tape, or paper clips. Finally, have students punch holes in the pouches and thread yarn or string through the holes, so the tooth totes can be worn as bracelets or necklaces, tied to belt loops or book bags, etc. When a student loses a tooth at school, let him store it and carry it home in his tooth tote. Also, give the student a copy of the Lost Tooth award (page 11) to display at his desk or at home!

Chomper Stomper

Students will bite off plenty of knowledge with this "chewing" activity. Using the jaw diagram (page 42) as a model, assign a different tooth to each student. If you have fewer students, form only the upper or lower jaw, or have students represent sets of teeth. Have students make a construction paper placard by drawing and cutting out the shape of the tooth they represent, and writing the tooth's name and function on the shape. Next, have students punch holes in the teeth, attach string or yarn, and wear the placards around their necks. Instruct students to line up in two facing semicircles, forming a correctly ordered upper and lower jaw. Now, ask students to demonstrate the cutting, tearing, and grinding functions of different teeth by pretending to "chew" different foods made from paper. For example, give the "incisors" a rolled up orange paper cone "carrot" and let them tear it apart the way front teeth would. Pass the carrot on to the cuspids on either side for more tearing and shredding, and finally, to the molars, who crush the "carrot" by balling up the paper tightly. Students can "swallow" food by dropping "chewed" objects into the "throat" of a waste basket.

40

toothbrush

toothpaste

dental floss

COPY and CUT

MILK MILK

milk carton

fingertip tooth patterns

incisor

cuspid

molar

The Primary Teeth

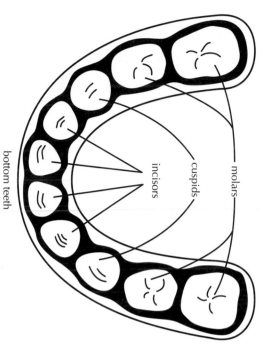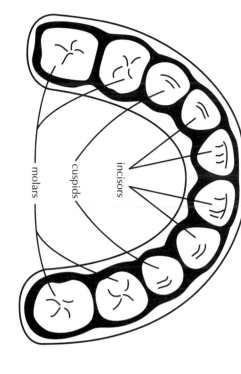

top teeth

bottom teeth

incisors
cuspids
molars

molars
cuspids
incisors

jaw diagram

- *Incisors are straight, sharp front teeth that cut food, like scissors cut paper.*

- *Cuspids, or canines, are pointed, fang-like teeth that tear food.*

- *Molars are wide back teeth that are used to crush and grind food.*

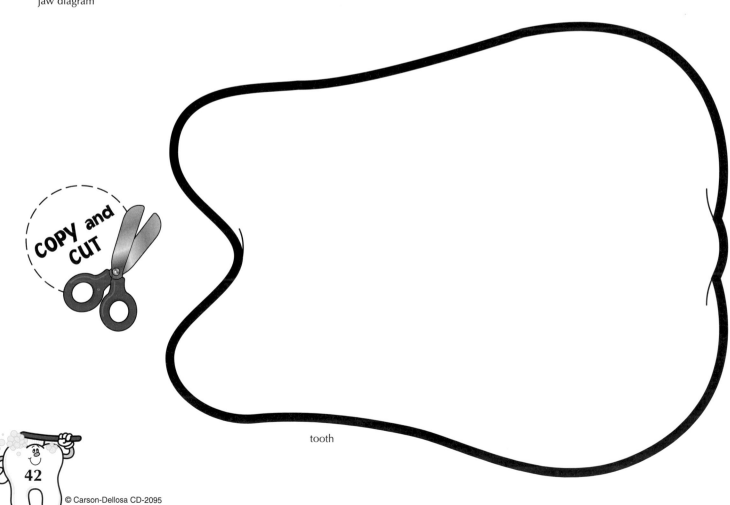

COPY and CUT

tooth

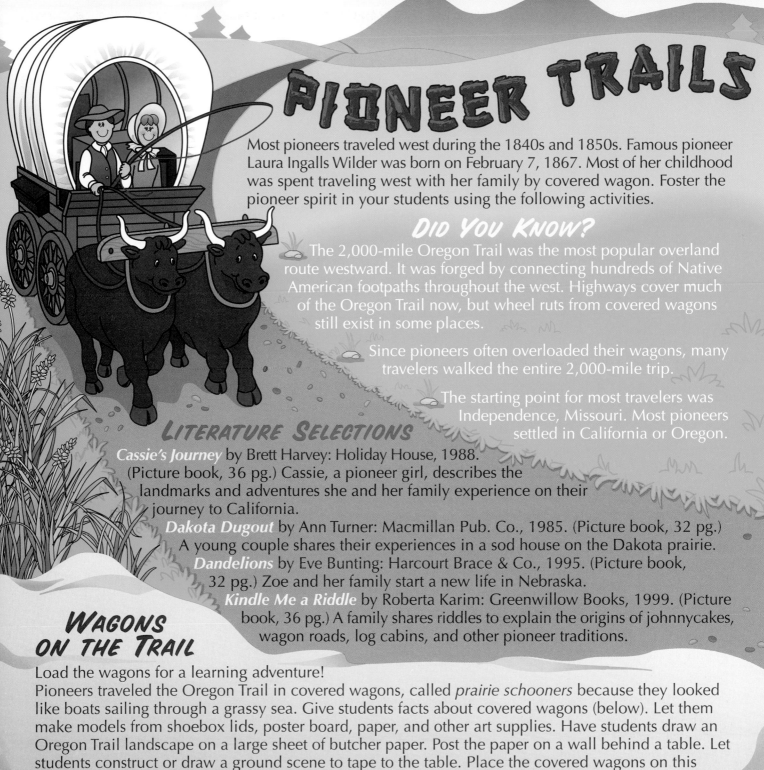

PIONEER TRAILS

Most pioneers traveled west during the 1840s and 1850s. Famous pioneer Laura Ingalls Wilder was born on February 7, 1867. Most of her childhood was spent traveling west with her family by covered wagon. Foster the pioneer spirit in your students using the following activities.

DID YOU KNOW?

The 2,000-mile Oregon Trail was the most popular overland route westward. It was forged by connecting hundreds of Native American footpaths throughout the west. Highways cover much of the Oregon Trail now, but wheel ruts from covered wagons still exist in some places.

Since pioneers often overloaded their wagons, many travelers walked the entire 2,000-mile trip.

The starting point for most travelers was Independence, Missouri. Most pioneers settled in California or Oregon.

LITERATURE SELECTIONS

Cassie's Journey by Brett Harvey: Holiday House, 1988. (Picture book, 36 pg.) Cassie, a pioneer girl, describes the landmarks and adventures she and her family experience on their journey to California.

Dakota Dugout by Ann Turner: Macmillan Pub. Co., 1985. (Picture book, 32 pg.) A young couple shares their experiences in a sod house on the Dakota prairie.

Dandelions by Eve Bunting: Harcourt Brace & Co., 1995. (Picture book, 32 pg.) Zoe and her family start a new life in Nebraska.

Kindle Me a Riddle by Roberta Karim: Greenwillow Books, 1999. (Picture book, 36 pg.) A family shares riddles to explain the origins of johnnycakes, wagon roads, log cabins, and other pioneer traditions.

WAGONS ON THE TRAIL

Load the wagons for a learning adventure!

Pioneers traveled the Oregon Trail in covered wagons, called *prairie schooners* because they looked like boats sailing through a grassy sea. Give students facts about covered wagons (below). Let them make models from shoebox lids, poster board, paper, and other art supplies. Have students draw an Oregon Trail landscape on a large sheet of butcher paper. Post the paper on a wall behind a table. Let students construct or draw a ground scene to tape to the table. Place the covered wagons on this classroom version of the Oregon Trail.

Covered Wagon Facts

- *Covered wagons were pulled by oxen. A yoke was attached to the front of the wagon to hold the oxen.*
- *Covered wagons had four wheels. The front two wheels were slightly smaller than the back two wheels.*
- *The wagon box, or bed, was made of wood.*
- *Sturdy wooden bows were bent across the top of the wagon to hold its cover.*
- *Boxes for supplies and equipment were often attached to the outsides of the wagons.*

43

PACK UP THE WAGON

Get students into the spirit and hardships of pioneering. Assign students to small groups and have them pretend to be pioneer families. Explain that pioneer families traveled west to start new lives, and had to transport any items they needed for their homes in their covered wagons. They had to take enough food for the five-month journey, tools to build their homes, household goods, and valuable personal items. Covered wagons could carry about 2,000 pounds. Anything heavier would break the wagons or would be too heavy for oxen to pull. Sometimes, families had to leave behind belongings when they crossed rivers or traveled over mountains. Give each "family" a copy of the Covered Wagon Supply List (page 50) and the covered wagon pattern (page 50). Have students cut around the wagon pattern top so it can be lifted up, then staple it to a sheet of paper. Have each family lift the wagon cover and list the items they would take on their journey, without exceeding 2,000 pounds. Ask families to explain which items they chose, and why.

SIGHTSEEING ALONG THE WAY

Teach students the skill of using landmarks! Few pioneers could have made it to their final destinations without using natural landmarks to tell how far they had traveled. The Oregon Trail stretched through plains, deserts, and mountains and took 5-6 months to travel. Many traveled in *wagon trains* (a single line of several covered wagons). Most wagon trains had a trail guide who had made the trip before and knew the landmarks. Many landmarks were rock formations, springs, or mountain passes with names describing their physical features. Enlarge and display the Oregon Trail map (page 51). Assign small groups and give each group a landmark to research, describe in writing, and illustrate. Have the groups label their landmarks on the map. Use yarn to attach the illustrations and descriptions to each landmark. Help the class trace the trail from beginning to end, and let each group describe its landmark.

OREGON TRAIL LANDMARKS
South Pass
Devil's Gate
Soda Springs
Chimney Rock
Independence Rock

THE OREGON TRAIL

Independence Rock

Chimney Rock

Soda Springs

INDEPENDENCE ROCK
Independence Rock was a large rock shaped like a turtle's back. A group of travelers celebrated Independence Day there.

CHIMNEY ROCK
Chimney Rock was a tall column that rose 500 feet into the sky. It looked like a huge chimney rising up from the ground.

SODA SPRINGS
Soda Springs was a body of bubbling water. Drinking water from the spring was like drinking soda.

44

A Day in a Pioneer's Life

Make sure students will remember their pioneer days by having them keep journals to reference facts they learn, recipes and crafts they make, and adventures they have while learning about pioneers. Many pioneers kept journals and diaries about their experiences traveling west. Some travelers wrote *reminiscences*—descriptions of their journeys written long after the trips. By reading these accounts, people are able to understand what the journey was like for the early settlers. To make a journal, give each child several enlarged copies of the covered wagon pattern (page 50). Have him color one pattern to use as a journal cover. During your study of pioneers, let each student write journal entries from a pioneer's point of view on the remaining patterns, then staple them under the cover.

My Pioneer Diary Sarah Powell

A "Hand"y Clock

Teach students to tell time the pioneer way—without a clock or watch! Westward-bound pioneers brought cows and other animals with them that roamed and grazed freely until pioneers settled and built barnyards. Some pioneer children were sent out at the end of each day to bring the grazing animals back to the homestead. To avoid getting lost after dark, pioneers used this technique to tell how much longer daylight would last. Find a place outside where students can see the sun and the horizon line. Have each student hold his arm out in front of him at eye level, elbow bent and palm facing inward. Instruct each child to place his hand between the bottom of the sun and the horizon. For every four fingers that fit between the horizon and the bottom of the sun, there should be one hour of daylight left. Each adult-sized finger represents approximately 15 minutes of daylight, so have students experiment with how far away their hands should be from their faces by comparing their time estimates to a clock.

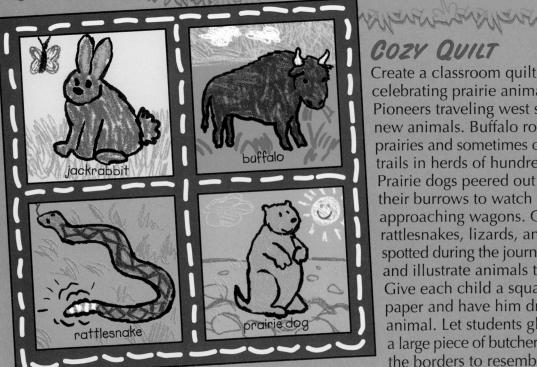

jackrabbit

buffalo

rattlesnake

prairie dog

Cozy Quilt

Create a classroom quilt celebrating prairie animals! Pioneers traveling west saw many new animals. Buffalo roamed the prairies and sometimes crossed the trails in herds of hundreds. Prairie dogs peered out from their burrows to watch the approaching wagons. Coyotes, jackrabbits, rattlesnakes, lizards, and antelope could also be spotted during the journeys. Have students research and illustrate animals that pioneers encountered. Give each child a square of construction paper and have him draw and label an animal. Let students glue their squares to a large piece of butcher paper and decorate the borders to resemble a quilt.

45

JUMPING JACK TOY

Because manufactured materials were scarce, pioneer children played with toys made from scraps of wood, fabric, and other natural materials. The jumping jack was a favorite. Let students make these toys using the jumping jack doll pattern (page 52). **1.** Copy and cut out the pieces from tagboard. Punch holes where large circles are shown on the patterns. Use a pushpin to punch smaller holes where the small circles are shown on the pieces. **2.** Cut and tie a loop of thread through the hole at the top of the pattern—this is used to hold the doll. **3.** Attach the arm and leg pieces with paper fasteners. **4.** Attach each arm and leg to the body with a paper fastener. Make sure arms and legs can swing freely. **5.** Turn the doll face down and straighten the arms and legs. Tie a piece of string through the two smaller holes in the shoulders. Tie another piece of string through the holes in the legs. **6.** Cut a 14" length of string. Tightly tie one end to the string that connects the arms. **7.** Run the string down and tightly tie it to the string connecting the legs. Allow the string to fall down to the doll's feet. **8.** Hold the loop above the doll's head in one hand, and hold the string at the bottom with the other hand. Pull the string to make the doll's arms and legs jump up and down!

CORN HUSK DOLLS

When settlers began to grow corn, they used the husks for fuel, to stuff mattresses, and even to make dolls! Have students use strips of brown grocery bags to make cornhusk dolls. **1.** Cut a 20" x 3" strip of paper from a grocery bag. Fold the strip in half lengthwise, with the fold at the top. **2.** Cut two 10" x 2" strips. Place the strips on top of each other and slide them about 3" below the fold to create arms. **3.** Crisscross a length of jute or raffia above and below the arms. Turn the large strip over and tie the ends of the jute in a knot. **4.** Tie short lengths of jute 2" from the end of each arm to create hands. **5.** To make a boy doll, cut the bottom into two strips and use jute to tie the pieces together in two groups to make pants. To make a girl doll, cut strips and let them hang loose to create a dress.

girl doll

boy doll

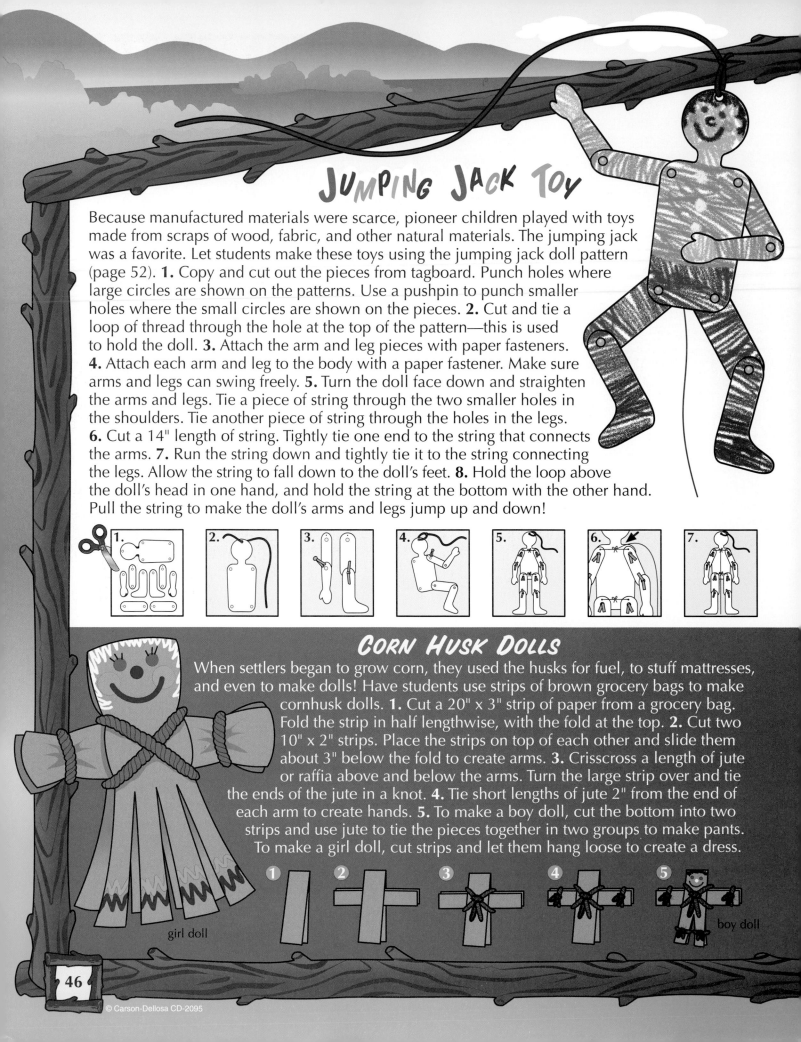

46

TASTY JOHNNYCAKES

Johnnycakes, a favorite pioneer food, were often served with maple syrup. Since they were easy to carry, johnnycakes were often eaten during the midday meal when pioneers were busy doing chores or tending crops.

JOHNNYCAKES

2 cups cornmeal
2 teaspoons salt
2 tablespoons butter
2 tablespoons sugar
2 cups boiling water
1 cup milk
vegetable oil
maple syrup

Mix the cornmeal, salt, butter, and sugar in a bowl. Add the boiling water and milk. Mix thoroughly with a spoon until the batter is thick. If the batter is too thick, add a little warm water. Heat the vegetable oil in a frying pan over medium heat. Drop batter by spoonfuls into the frying pan. Cook for about five minutes on each side until crisp and brown. Serve with maple syrup. Makes about 16 johnnycakes.

BUBBLING SODA CONCOCTION

Europeans and Americans alike discovered that some natural springs contained carbonated water–just like the water found in modern soda! Because these springs were hard to find, innovators found ways to make water "fizzy." Pioneers made carbonated drinks from their own recipes, like this one.

INGREDIENTS

Sugar syrup:
tap water
2 cups sugar
1/4 teaspoon vanilla extract

Soda pop:
sugar syrup
assorted fruit juices *(for flavoring)*
1 small bottle lemon juice
1 small box baking soda
(makes about 16 four-ounce servings)

Directions

First, make sugar syrup. Heat two cups of water, add sugar, and stir until dissolved. Add vanilla. Remove syrup from heat and allow to cool. Pour the mixture into a large jar and chill in the refrigerator.

To make one serving of soda, pour four ounces of cold water into a large glass. Add one tablespoon of sugar syrup, 1/4 teaspoon baking soda, 1/4 teaspoon lemon juice, and fruit juice to taste. Stir well and serve over ice.

47

LIFE IN A PIONEER HOME

Pioneers usually built one of two kinds of homes—log cabins and sod houses. Share the information below with students. Let each student do research, then draw a log cabin on one sheet of paper and a sod house on another. Staple a piece of white paper under each picture and have students cut around the outlines. On the bottom sheets, let students illustrate the hearths, furniture, and other items inside each home. Compare the homes and ask students which they would prefer to build, and why.

LIFE IN A LOG CABIN

When pioneers settled on land with trees, they cleared fields for crops then used the trees to build log cabins. They cut notches in the ends of the logs so they would fit together, and stuffed mud or moss between them to keep out rain and cold. Roofs, and sometimes floors, were built from wide wooden planks with wooden peg fasteners. Tables, chairs, and beds were also made from split logs. Small windows were covered with greased paper or animal skins. A stone hearth was built in the kitchen for cooking and warmth. Some cabins had a loft, accessible by ladder, where children slept on mattresses stuffed with dried leaves or grass. Clothing and household items were hung from pegs.

LIFE IN A SOD HOUSE

Settlers who lived on open prairie without trees built sod houses. To make the walls, pioneers cut and stacked blocks of sod or hard ground like bricks. Plant roots in the sod bricks were left to grow together to keep the bricks in place. Some houses had a few windows that were covered with greased paper to keep the rain out. Floors were dirt and roofs were thatch or grass-covered. The inner walls of sod houses were covered with newspaper or canvas to protect them from drafts. Leather or canvas covered the doorway. Sod houses had stoves inside where grass was burned for warmth and cooking. Settlers used furniture they brought with them in their covered wagons.

BRAIDING A RUG

To make log cabins and sod houses seem more like homes, and to keep floors warm during winter months, pioneers made braided rugs from old strips of fabric. Have students work in pairs to make miniature versions of braided rugs, using fabric scraps. Let each student cut three strips of fabric 18" long and 1" wide. Stack the strips and tie them together using heavy thread. Have one student hold the strips at the tied end while the other tightly braids the strips together. Use quilting thread to tie off the finished braided piece. Then, have each child spread glue over a piece of paper and coil the braided piece into a rug on top of the glue. The glue will hold the coil in place. Have students draw pioneer home scenes around the rugs.

PIONEER POTTERY

Because they were breakable, few crocks and jugs for food storage were carried in wagons. When pioneer families settled in a new home, they made their own pottery by shaping clay found in creeks and river beds, hardening the pieces over an open fire to make earthenware. Provide self-hardening clay and let students make clay crocks. Instruct each student to make a small, flat circle for the base of the crock, then roll the remaining clay into long ropes. Layer the ropes on top of each other until the crock is the desired height, and use a craft stick to smooth the seams on the inside and outside of the crock. Attach two clay rope pieces to make handles. Allow the clay to dry. Have students decorate the pottery using acrylic paint.

PIONEER SPELLING BEE

Learn spelling the old-fashioned way with a spelling bee. Explain that few pioneer communities had schools. Most children were taught at home. When a town grew large enough, residents built a schoolhouse. One teacher usually taught reading, penmanship, and math to children of all ages. To teach spelling, schools frequently held classroom spelling bees, in which two teams took turns spelling words read aloud by the teacher. Students who misspelled words were out of the game, and the remaining student won. Winning a spelling bee was a great achievement and sometimes community spelling bees were held. To hold a pioneer-themed class spelling bee, give each child several index cards on which to write pioneer words like wagon, johnnycake, log cabin, Oregon Trail, embroidery, skillet, oxen, churn, caravan, frontier, journey, etc. Collect the cards and divide the class into two groups. Read the students' words and have them take turns spelling them aloud.

WORKING AND PLAYING TOGETHER

After all the hard work, let your students celebrate with music, just like pioneers! Pioneer families worked together to build homes and barns, harvest food, and make necessities like quilts and candles. Pioneers celebrated the completion of work with harvest or barn parties that included music, dancing, and games. When harmonicas, guitars, drums, and other instuments were not available, they made them from gourds, pieces of wood, and string. Let students create a homemade standing bass from cans and thread. Have an adult use a hammer and nail to punch holes in the bottoms of large coffee cans. Let each student measure and cut a length of heavy thread reaching from the floor to his waist. Tie a button to one end of the thread and push it through the can, so the button is on the inside. Tie the other end of the thread around the middle of an unsharpened pencil. Have each child play his bass by placing the can open-side down on the floor and placing one foot on top of the can, while holding the pencil. Have him use his other hand to pluck the thread to create sounds. Loosen or tighten the thread to change the pitch.

COVERED WAGON SUPPLY LIST

TOOLS & HOUSEHOLD ITEMS

ax	15	pounds
shovel	15	pounds
hammer	8	pounds
rope	5	pounds
hoe	5	pounds
saw	12	pounds
nails	20	pounds
spinning wheel	100	pounds
candles	5	pounds
butter churn	25	pounds
lantern	5	pounds
coffee grinder	4	pounds
cooking utensils	20	pounds
pots and pans	50	pounds
trunk	40	pounds
dishes	30	pounds
kettle	40	pounds
buckets	15	pounds
plow	60	pounds
seeds	5	pounds
rugs	20	pounds
blankets/quilts	50	pounds
scissors	1	pound

FOOD

flour	150	pounds
coffee	100	pounds
bacon	50	pounds
salt pork	50	pounds
dried beans	100	pounds
salt	100	pounds
sugar	40	pounds
water	300	pounds
oatmeal	50	pounds
spices	10	pounds
dried fruit	20	pounds
cornmeal	45	pounds
tea	30	pounds

PERSONAL ITEMS

cloth	20	pounds
needles/thread/pins	2	pounds
doll	2	pounds
marbles	1	pound
books	5	pounds
fiddle	2	pounds
rifle	10	pounds
hunting knife	2	pounds
winter coats	25	pounds
boots/snowshoes	10	pounds
shoes	10	pounds
mirror	20	pounds
grandfather clock	200	pounds
table and chairs	300	pounds

covered wagon supply list

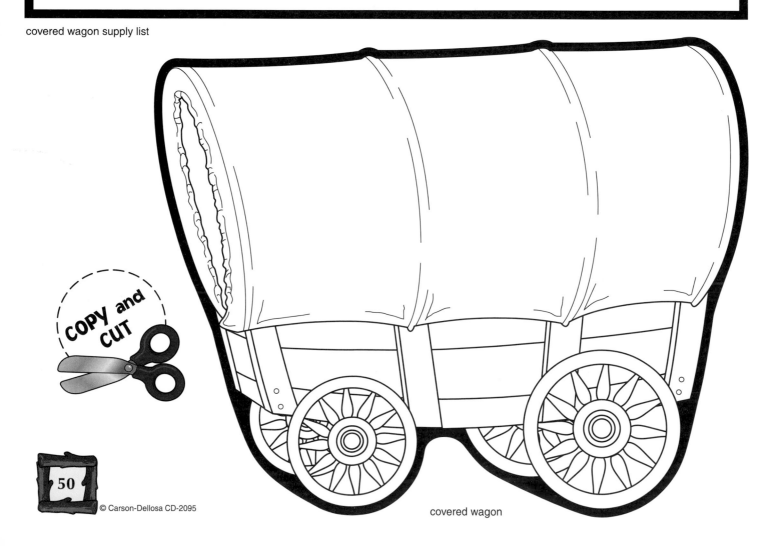

COPY and CUT

covered wagon

THE OREGON TRAIL

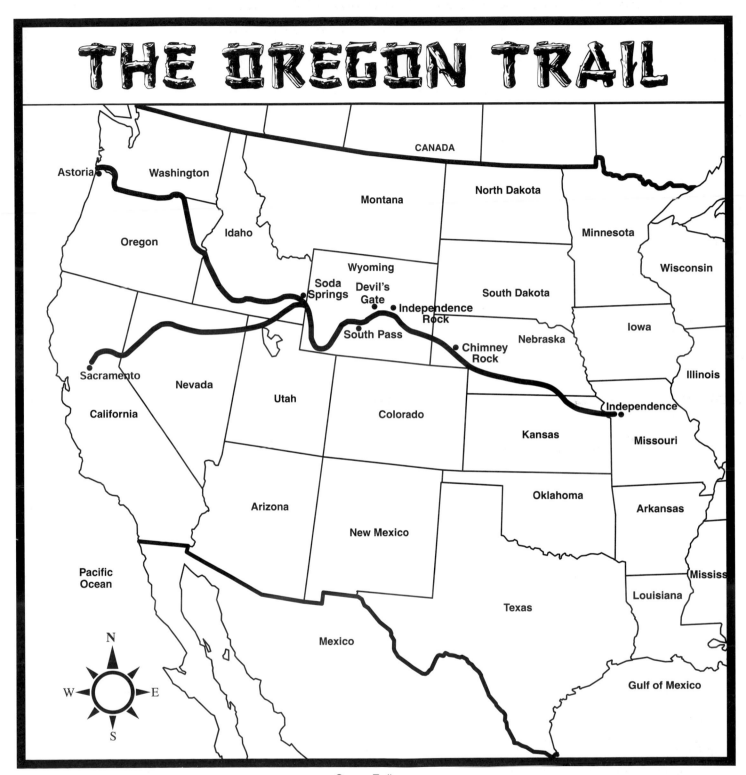

Oregon Trail map

★Map reflects current state and country borders.

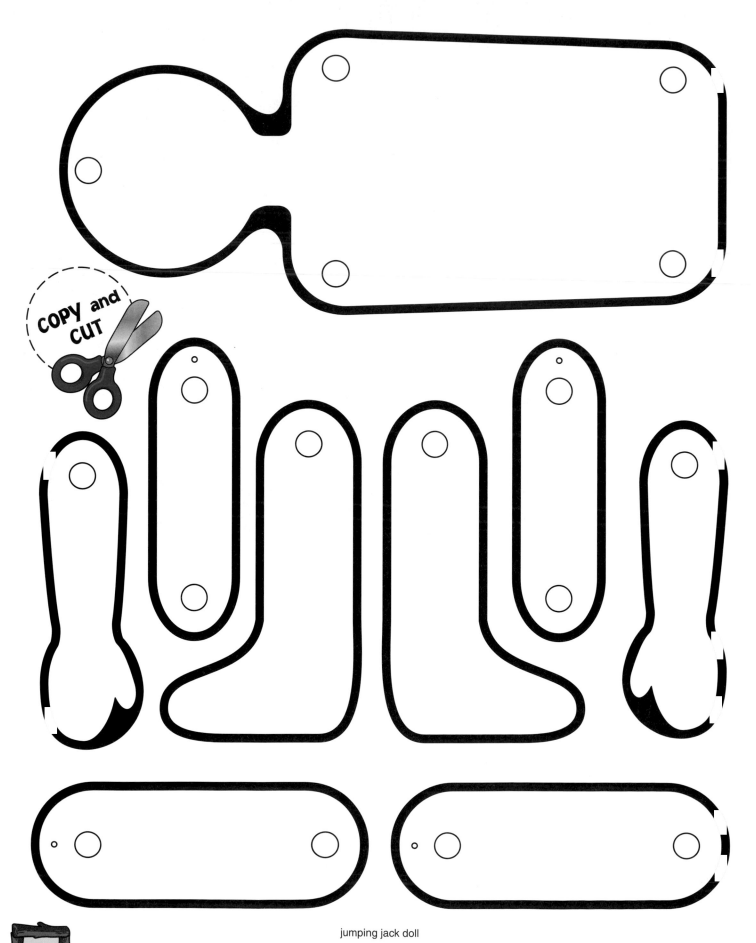

COPY and CUT

jumping jack doll

Thomas Edison
American Inventor

Thomas Alva Edison was born February 11, 1847, and became one of the United States' most famous and important inventors. He is responsible for making electricity and light available to homes and businesses. In February, celebrate the birthday of the most prolific inventor of our times, Thomas Edison.

Did You Know?

- During his lifetime, Edison was granted a record 1,093 U.S. patents.
- The phonograph was Edison's favorite invention. When he replayed a recording of himself reciting *Mary Had a Little Lamb*, it worked the very first time.
- Edison is famous for saying, "Genius is 1% inspiration and 99% perspiration."
- Edison continually sketched and took notes about new ideas and inventions, filling 3,400 notebooks in his lifetime.

Literature Selections

Thomas Edison and Electricity by Steve Parker: Chelsea House, 1995. (Nonfiction book, 32 pg.)

Perseverance!: The Story of Thomas Alva Edison by Peter Murray: The Child's World, Incorporated, 1997. (Nonfiction book, 32 pg.)

The Story of Thomas Alva Edison, Inventor: The Wizard of Menlo Park by Margaret Davidson: Scholastic, Inc., 1990. (Nonfiction book, 64 pg.)

Cooperative Biography

Illuminate Thomas Edison's life and inventions. Divide the class into eight groups and assign each group an aspect of Edison's life and work to research—see below for a partial list of topics. Have each group write a report, draw a picture, and create a title page for their topic. Bind the reports together to make a biography for students to read and learn about Thomas Alva Edison.

- Childhood: schooling, first job, printing own newspaper
- Young adulthood: telegraph operator, marriage
- Early inventions: vote recorder, stock ticker, electric pen
- Invention factory and Menlo Park
- Phonograph
- Incandescent lighting: lightbulb, electric company
- Kinetoscope
- Later years: fluoroscope, alkaline battery, source of rubber

 53

The Invention Factory

Thomas Edison established the first "invention factory." There, he and his workers, called *muckers*, worked to improve existing products and create practical inventions. Let students pretend to be Edison's muckers, and create their own invention factory by finding ways to make things more useful. Brainstorm a list of existing products such as cars, microwaves, computers, and televisions. Have students work in groups to discuss how these products could be made more useful. Could "Travelvision" transport people to places on a television screen? Encourage groups to sketch and take notes on their ideas, as Edison did, then present them to the class. Discuss what patents are, and why they are needed. Let students create and fill out mock patent certificates and display them beside their inventions.

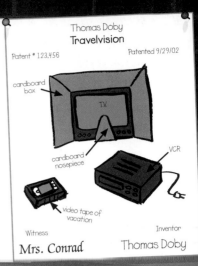

Perseverance Pays Off

Phonograph
Electric company
Rubber from goldenrod
Stock ticker
Electric pen
Vote counter
Electric lamp
Railroad powered by electricty
Alkaline storage battery
kiNetograph
Carbon transmitter
Electric miner's lamp

After many failed attempts to develop a battery, Edison said, "We've made a lot of progress. At least we know 8,000 things that won't work." Show the fruits of Edison's perseverance with this display of his inventions. Have each child write the word PERSEVERANCE vertically on a sheet of paper. Challenge each to list one of Edison's inventions for each letter. Some need not start with the letter, but may include that letter in the word. Enlarge the lightbulb pattern (page 56) for each child and have him rewrite his acrostic on the pattern. Display the lightbulbs on a bulletin board with the title *Edison's Perseverance Paid Off!*

A Groovy Invention

Let students observe and report on Edison's favorite invention, the phonograph. Bring in phonograph records. Allow students to observe the grooves in the vinyl and make rubbings on paper with pencils or crayons. Play a record and have students observe the needle moving up and down as it passes over the grooves. Challenge students to write a newspaper article about the phonograph and how it works, as if they are living in Edison's time and have just seen the phonograph for the first time.

The original phonograph consisted of a grooved cylinder covered by tin foil, turned by a hand crank. A person would talk into a disk near the cylinder, causing a needle on the bottom of the disk to vibrate, indenting the foil. When the needle was dragged backwards over the same grooves, the process reversed and the sounds played back. The indented foil cylinder was eventually replaced by a grooved vinyl disk, which was more durable and produced better sound quality.

Moving Pictures

Experiment with the phenomena called *persistence of vision* that led Edison to develop the kinetoscope, an early movie camera and viewer. Persistence of vision exists because the brain keeps an image for an instant after it is gone. By rapidly viewing a series of slightly different pictures, or frames, the object in the pictures seems to move. Let students use this principle to make a flip book. Have each student cut out ten 3" squares from heavy paper and staple them together at the top. Starting with the last page, draw a slightly different picture on each page of the book. For example, to show a figure walking left to right, draw the first frame (on the back page) with the figure at the far left. Draw the figure in the next frame (the next-to-last page) slightly right; the next frame a little more right, and so on until the last frame (top page) shows the figure "starting" at the far right of the page. To view the "movie," quickly flip the pages from bottom to top with the thumb.

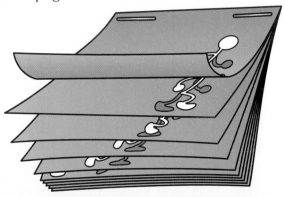

A Bright Idea!

Edison is most famous for inventing the lightbulb, but he also invented lamps, switches, and a power station. If possible, invite someone from an electric company to talk about where and how electricity is generated, and how it gets to homes and businesses. Explain that lightbulbs today look similar to Edison's. Provide a clear lightbulb and a lightbulb pattern (page 56) for each child, and have her draw on the pattern what she observes inside the bulb. Next, let students go full circuit and light real bulbs. Cut apart bulbs from a string of small, white holiday lights, leaving about 3" of wire on each side, and carefully strip the coating from the ends of the wires. Give students one AA battery and a holiday light. Instruct students to touch one wire to each end of the battery, completing the circuit and illuminating the lightbulb. This will not shock students, but will surely spark their imaginations!

Secret Code

Students can try to encode and decode secret Morse code messages, just like Edison! As a young man, Edison worked as a telegraph operator. He said his hearing loss helped him block out other sounds and concentrate on the high pitched dots and dashes. He talked secretly to his wife by tapping Morse code messages on her hand. He even nicknamed his first two children "Dot" and "Dash." Pair students and give each a copy of the Morse code chart (page 56). Allow children to refer to the chart while one child taps out a message to the other on her hand, one letter at a time. Challenge the other child to write down the letters as they are tapped out to decode the secret message. Let partners trade places and try the activity again.

55

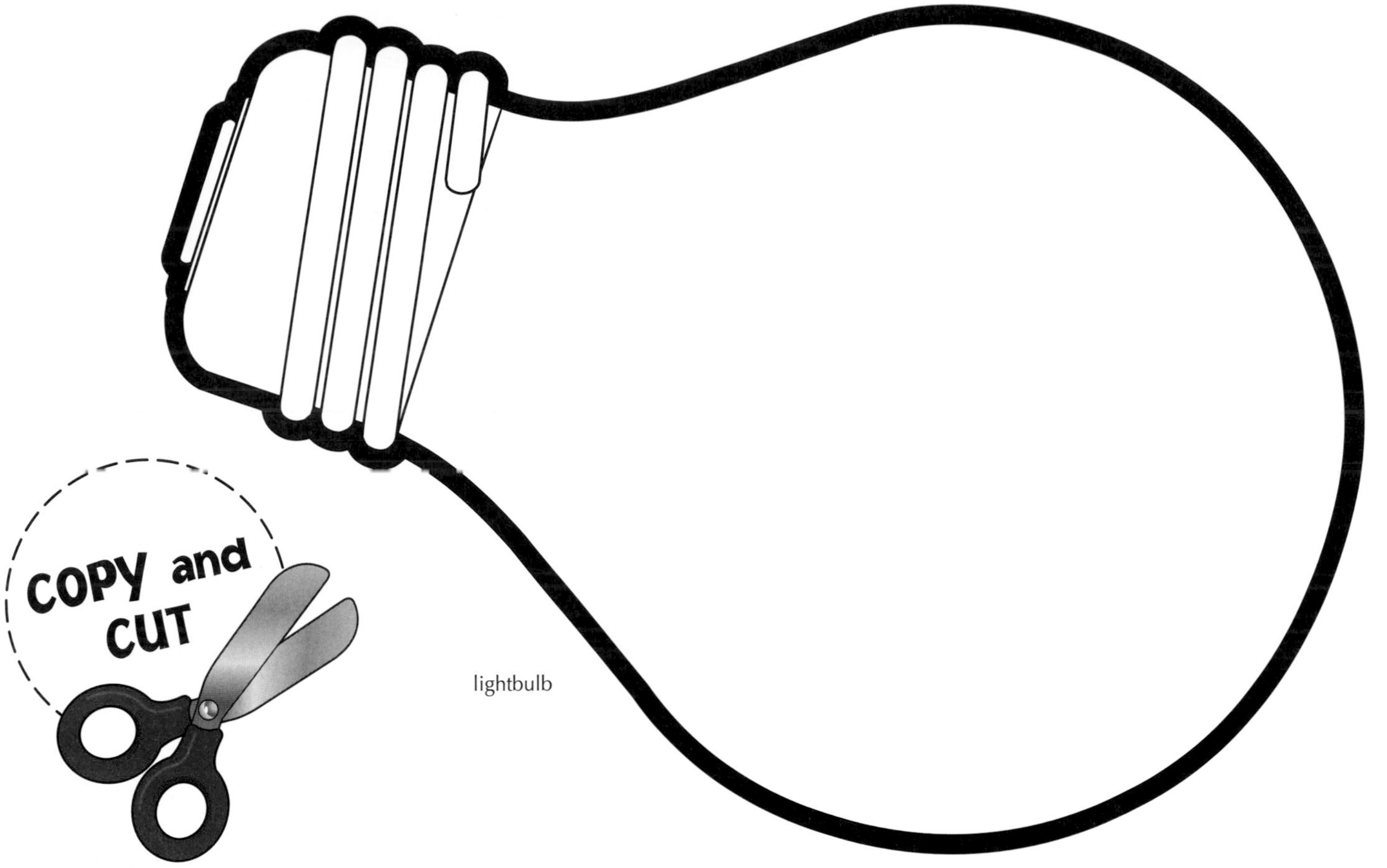

COPY and CUT

lightbulb

International Morse Code

A ·—	J ·———	S ···	
B —···	K —·—	T —	
C —·—·	L ·—··	U ··—	
D —··	M ——	V ···—	
E ·	N —·	W ·——	
F ··—·	O ———	X —··—	
G ——·	P ·——·	Y —·——	
H ····	Q ——·—	Z ——··	
I ··	R ·—·		
Period ·—·—·—	Comma ——··——		
Question Mark ··——··	Error ········		

56

Morse code chart

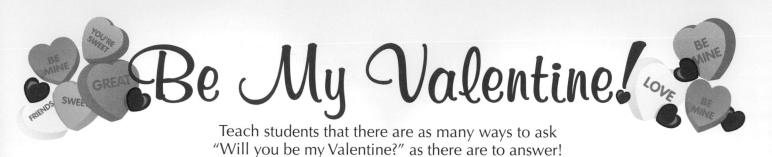

Be My Valentine!

Teach students that there are as many ways to ask
"Will you be my Valentine?" as there are to answer!

Did You Know?

♥ No one knows exactly how Valentine's Day began. Some Valentine's Day traditions probably came from the ancient Roman festival *Lupercalia*, which honored Juno, the goddess of marriage.

♥ Another legend claims that St. Valentine, a Roman priest, was especially popular with young couples because he performed their wedding ceremonies, even though the Roman government discouraged marriage at the time.

♥ The oldest Valentine still in existence is a poem written in England by the Duke of Orleans, in 1415, to his wife. The poem is on display at the British Museum in London.

Literature Selections

Cranberry Valentine by Wende Devlin: Aladdin, 1992. (Picture book, 36 pg.) Maggie and her grandmother send secret valentines to Mr. Whiskers.

Junie B. Jones and the Mushy Gushy Valentine by Barbara Park: Random House, 1999. (Storybook, 80 pg.) Junie B. cannot believe it when a secret admirer sends a mushy valentine to her!

Roses are Pink, Your Feet Really Stink! by Diane deGroat: Mulberry Books, 1997. (Picture book, 32 pg.) Gilbert learns how to write nice valentine cards, even when he'd rather not.

"My Heart Beats for You" Cards

The heart shape is a popular Valentine symbol of love and emotion. Help children follow the steps below to make beating heart cards to symbolize the organ's function. Each child will need a sheet of 5" x 7" card stock, two ½" x 4" strips of card stock, a sheet of red or pink construction paper, scissors, and art supplies.

1. Cut a heart shape from construction paper. Decorate and add a Valentine slogan. Cut the heart in half.
2. Place the heart halves together on the sheet of card stock. On the card stock, mark where the top and bottom of the heart halves line up.
3. Glue one card stock strip to the back of each heart half as shown.
4. Cut four slots into the card stock, each about 2" long (students may need help with this step).
5. Slide the strips through the slits to make the heart "beat."

57

Make & Shake Cards

Children will enjoy making and shaking these unusual cards. Have each child fold an 8½" x 5½" piece of red construction paper in half, then unfold it. Trace and cut out a heart shape from one side of the paper. Sprinkle confetti on the other side, then cover it with a piece of cellophane larger than the heart. Glue the edges of the cellophane to seal in the confetti. When the glue is dry, glue the inside edges of the card together. Punch two holes in the top of the card. Thread and tie a decorative ribbon through the holes.

♡ Pinprick Valentines ♡

Early handmade valentines were often very elaborate. One type, called a *pinprick* valentine, resembled paper lace. Let each child make a simple, light pencil drawing with a Valentine's Day theme on construction paper. Then, let children tape the papers to cardboard and use pushpins to punch holes in the paper along the outline of the drawing. Remove the drawings from the cardboard and display them over yellow or red paper, or in a window to let light shine through the designs.

Pop-Out Valentines

Valentines with pop-out decorations became popular in 19th-century England. Follow the diagrams to make valentines with surprises inside!

1. Give each child two colors of card stock. Cut two parallel slits about 2" long in one piece of card stock to create a tab.
2. Fold the two sheets of card stock together. Pull the tab in the center out from the fold. Glue the edges of the card stock together, leaving the tab unglued.
3. Cut out a paper heart and write a valentine message on it. Attach the heart to the bottom of the tab, so it is flat when the card is closed. When the card is opened, the heart pops out!

Special Envelopes for Special Valentines

Make envelopes as pretty as the cards they carry! Provide copies of the envelope pattern (page 66) enlarged to different sizes. Each child should choose an envelope pattern slightly larger than the card to be mailed. Let each child trace the pattern on the back of wrapping paper, then follow the pattern instructions to fold and tape the wrapping paper to make an envelope. Use the envelopes to deliver *Make & Shake Valentines*, *Pinprick Valentines*, or *Pop-Out Valentines* (see above).

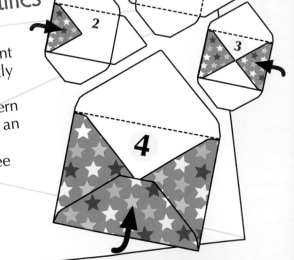

58

Sealed with a Stamp

Brighten existing envelopes with special seals. Explain that before envelopes were made with adhesive flaps, people dripped hot wax on envelope flaps. Sometimes a ring with a special design was pressed into the wax. The recipient of the letter knew no one else had read the letter if the wax was intact. Let students make special valentine seals using raw potato halves. Help students use a paper clip end to scratch a heart shape in a potato. Older students can carve their initials into the heart shape as well. Assist students in cutting around the heart using a dinner knife, so that the heart is raised. Combine different paint colors on each heart to form individual stamps. Let students stamp their "seals" on the flaps of sealed envelopes.

Heart-Shaped Doilies

Add interest to cut-out heart cards with lacy borders. Paper lace was accidentally invented when London paper maker Joseph Addenbrooke pushed a sharp metal file over paper embossed with a raised design. The file sheared off the raised design, leaving tiny, lace-like holes in the paper.

Make lace doilies the easy way!

1. Cut a large heart from white construction paper.
2. Fold the heart in half, then fold up the pointed bottom even with the folded side.
3. Fold the lower right edge up and left so the left edges are parallel.
4. Fold the rounded edge down over the straight edge.
5. Cut several notches in the heart as if making a paper snowflake, then unfold the doily. Glue the doily behind a smaller, solid paper heart with a special valentine message written on it.

 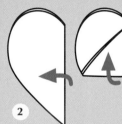   

You're Special!

Assembly Line Valentines

In 1848, Esther Howland, the daughter of a stationer, designed valentine cards from paper lace and flowers. The cards were so popular that she had to create an assembly line to meet the demand. She designed the cards and other workers copied her design. One added lace, another added beads, etc. Create a class Valentine assembly line. Use the valentine patterns (page 66) to make a model for students to follow. Assign students to write messages, add glitter, etc. Have students sign the cards, then choose a place to send your assembly line valentines, such as a retirement center or children's hospital.

59

👁 ❤ Rebus Books!

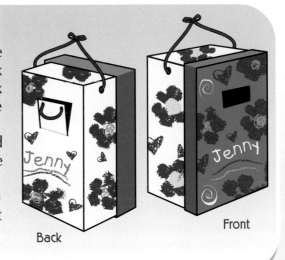

Valentines are more fun when there is a puzzle inside! Rebus valentines, which deliver their messages with pictures, were popular in the 1700's. Practice making rebus sentences. Have students fold a few sheets of construction paper in half, then cut along the fold to make heart-shaped pages. Unfold the pages and punch several holes along the left side. Explain the concept of a rebus sentence and brainstorm words which can be easily represented with pictures. Compound words (*treehouse, sunflower, rainbow, etc.*) make good choices. Begin each page with the rebus version of the sentence *I love...* by gluing on an eye cut from a magazine and a construction paper heart. Students can complete the rebus sentences with pictures of things they love. To complete each book, stack the pages together, thread ribbon through the punched holes, then tie beads to the ribbon ends to hold them in place. Have students try to decipher each others' sentences.

Valentine Mailboxes

Hanging mailboxes will keep students' desks clutter free. Provide a shoebox for each child. Tape the lid to the box. Stand each box on its short side. Assist each child in cutting a mail slot in the box lid, and a square, pull-down flap in the box bottom. Pull out the flap in the box bottom and punch two holes in the top left and right corners of the flap. Tie a ribbon handle through the punched holes. Then, punch a hole in each side of the box, and tie a piece of string through the holes. Let children add their names to the mailboxes, and decorate them. For Valentine mail delivery, loop the string over the back of each child's chair, so the mailbox slot faces out. Children can pull down the flaps in the backs of the boxes to retrieve delivered mail.

Back   Front

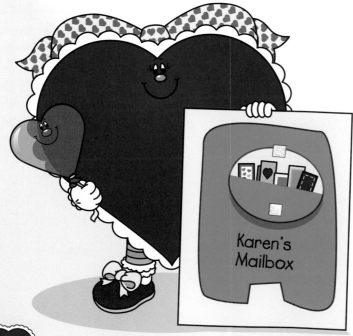

Flat Mailboxes

This space-saving box is perfect for delivering a small number of valentines. Give each child a copy of the drop mailbox pattern (page 67) on card stock. Have children cut out the patterns and decorate the mailboxes with their names, then cut along the dotted line to make a mailbox flap. Glue each pattern on an 8$\frac{1}{2}$" x 11" sheet of card stock (do not put glue behind the flap). Finally, attach self-adhesive hook tape to the back of the flap and to the card stock underneath. As children create valentines for their families, they can open the flaps and slide their cards into their mailboxes for safekeeping until they take them home.

For more mailbox and envelope ideas, refer to the Post Office chapter (pages 74-78).

When in Rome...

Double the Valentine's Day fun with this Roman tradition!
Explain that Roman children drew names from jars to see
who would be their partners for the *Lupercalia* festival (see
Did You Know?, page 57). Give markers and slips of paper
to half of the students. Have students print their names on the
slips, then fold them and place them in a jar. Allow each student
to draw a name from the jar to see who will be his partner. Let
partners sit together for a day or work together on assignments. You
may want to complete the process more than once so that each child
can write his name on a slip of paper and draw a name from the jar.

Advice for Cupid

Use valentine story starters to sharpen students' problem-
solving skills. Explain that in Greek and Roman
mythology, it was Cupid's job to make people fall in
love by shooting them with an invisible, painless arrow.
On enlarged copies of the cupid stationery (page 68),
write funny questions from Cupid, as if the cherub is
asking for advice. Examples might be: *Cupid needs a
vacation. Where would be the best place for Cupid to
relax?* or *Cupid is tired of using arrows. What could
Cupid use instead, and how would he use it?* Place the
cards in a horizontal row across the top of a bulletin
board. Let each child choose a story starter and write
a letter of advice to Cupid on copies of the stationery.
Post the letters on the bulletin board, then let children
read their letters aloud.

A Picture is Worth a Thousand Words

Students can frame "sweet" portraits
for their families. Use an instant
camera to photograph each student.
Have students glue four craft sticks
together to create a square frame
about the size of the photograph.
Then, let students glue conversation
hearts or cinnamon candy hearts to
the front of the craft stick frame.
Next, secure the front of the photo
to the back of the frame by gluing
it around the edges. Glue a loop of
string to the back of the photograph
for hanging.

A Valentine Party!

Reward students for their hard valentine work with these treats and activities to celebrate Valentine's Day.

Valentine Words

How many words can you make from the letters in the word *valentine*? To keep students occupied during the waiting period before their Valentine's Day party, pass out copies of the valentine worksheet (page 65) for them to complete. Offer prizes to the students who think of the most words, names, nouns, verbs, etc.

What's Red All Over?

A few days before your Valentine's Day party, tell students that red is the traditional color of valentines. Ask students to wear as much red as they can on the day of the party. Give everyone a prize for participating. Let students vote on who should receive an extra prize for wearing the most red, the most unusual red clothing item, the most heart shapes on a piece of clothing, etc.

Heart Cakes

Make these heart-shaped cupcakes without heart-shaped pans. First, prepare a cake mix according to package directions. Place cupcake liners in a muffin tin, then add the batter. Before baking, place a ceramic pie weight or a marble between the pan and the side of each liner to create a dent in each cupcake. When the baked cupcakes are pulled from the wrappers, they will be heart-shaped! Let students decorate the cupcakes with colored frosting and valentine-themed candy sprinkles.

Mmm...Smooth!

These tasty smoothies are a welcome break from the sugary sweetness of most valentine treats! Provide 1 pound frozen strawberries (reserve a few for garnish), 4 cups pineapple juice, 1 cup orange juice, and 1 1/2 cups vanilla yogurt. Mix the ingredients in stages in a blender until you have a smooth, thick drink. Slice the reserved strawberries vertically—they will be somewhat heart-shaped! If desired, cut a small slit in the bottom of a fresh strawberry and place it on the rim of the cup. Give each child a small cup of smoothie with a garnish.

Lollipop Valentine Cookies

Children can devour these cookies in class or wrap them in colorful plastic to take home. Provide refrigerated sugar cookie dough and craft sticks (one per child). Soak the craft sticks in water for at least an hour before this activity. Let students roll out the dough on sheets of waxed paper until it is 1/8" thick. Let each child cut two 3" heart shapes from the dough using a cookie cutter. Chill the dough in the freezer for one hour. Five minutes before the cookies finish chilling, remove the craft sticks from the water and pat them dry. Place half of the hearts on baking sheets. Let each student place a craft stick in the center of one cookie cutout so that 2 1/2" of the craft stick is a handle, then place a second cookie on top of each handle, pressing the edges to seal. Bake the cookies according to package directions. When the cookies are cooled, lift them off the baking sheet with a spatula. Let children decorate the cookies with colored sugar, melted chocolate (from the *Solid, Liquid, Delicious!* activity, page 64), or sprinkles.

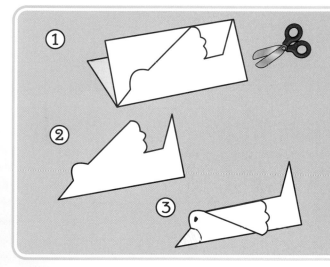

Flying Love Doves

Explain that doves are symbols of peace and love, then play this indoor/outdoor game at your valentine party. First, trace and cut out a template from the dove pattern (page 68) on heavy paper or cardstock. **1.** Give each student an 8 1/2" x 11" sheet of paper and have her fold it in half lengthwise. Instruct students to trace the dove pattern along the folded edge. **2.** Have them cut out the dove with the paper still folded. **3.** Add and color a beak and eyes, and then fold down the wings. Make sure you have plenty of space, then have contests to see whose doves fly the farthest!

Musical Cards

This holiday version of musical chairs can be played in small groups or as a class. Have each student cut out one heart shape from construction paper. Only one heart should be red; the other hearts should be different colors. Pass out slips of paper and instruct students to write a silly activity or question on each slip. For example: *If you had to choose new colors for Valentine's Day, what would they be?*; *What food should everyone have to eat on Valentine's Day?*; *Sing "Happy Valentine's Day to You"* to the teacher; etc. Place the slips in a jar. Have students sit in a circle, holding their heart shapes. Play music as the children pass the hearts around the circle. When the music stops, the child with the red heart must draw a slip, then answer the question or perform the activity. Discard slips as they are drawn, and play until all slips have been used.

63

Candy Connections

What would Valentine's Day be without candy? Use these delicious activities to satisfy every sweet tooth.

Love is Like a Chocolate Rose

Chocolate roses can be better than the real thing! Give each child two chocolate covered cherries or other chocolates, red or pink plastic wrap, green tissue paper, and a green pipe cleaner. Instruct them to place the chocolates bottom-to-bottom, then wrap them with plastic wrap to make a "rosebud." Tape the plastic wrap in place. Place the end of a pipe cleaner against the chocolates, and wrap tape around the "stem" to attach it to the "bud." Tape green paper leaves to the pipe cleaner. Let each child make several chocolate roses to create a bouquet.

Candy Messages

Use candy conversation hearts or candy bar wrappers for this mouth-watering activity. Assemble candy hearts or wrappers with different sayings. Challenge the class to make up sentences and stories using the words on the candy or wrappers. For example, a sentence using candy bar wrappers might read, *I* Snickered *when I saw the astronaut leave* Mars *to fly through the* Milky Way (from *Snickers®*, *Mars®*, and *Milky Way®* candy bars). On poster board, write out the sentences, gluing the corresponding hearts or wrappers to the poster board in the correct spaces.

Solid, Liquid, Delicious!

Explore the sweet science of chocolate. Supply waxed paper, resealable plastic bags, chocolate or white chocolate chips, fruit, stick pretzels, and plastic forks. Place the chocolate in a pan, and give each child a chocolate chip to taste. Ask students how they know the chocolate is a solid. (It is firm to the touch and holds its shape). Melt the chocolate over low heat or in a microwave. Let children watch you stir the chocolate. How do they know it is now a liquid? (It takes the shape of the bowl.) Pour warm chocolate into plastic bags, snip off a corner of each bag, and let children write and draw on waxed paper by squeezing chocolate out of the bag. While the chocolate designs are cooling, let the children dunk the fruit and pretzels into the warm chocolate in the pan. When children revisit their waxed paper creations, they should find that their drawings are solidifying, just in time to peel and eat!

Name _____

Use the letters in the word Valentine to make new words. Write the words below.

VALENTINE

_____   _____

_____   _____

_____   _____

_____   _____

_____   _____

_____   _____

_____   _____

_____   _____

_____   _____

_____   _____

Quick-and-Easy Valentine Cards

Enlarge these valentine patterns for the Assembly Line Valentines activity (page 59), for students to color, or copy them on construction paper to give to students.

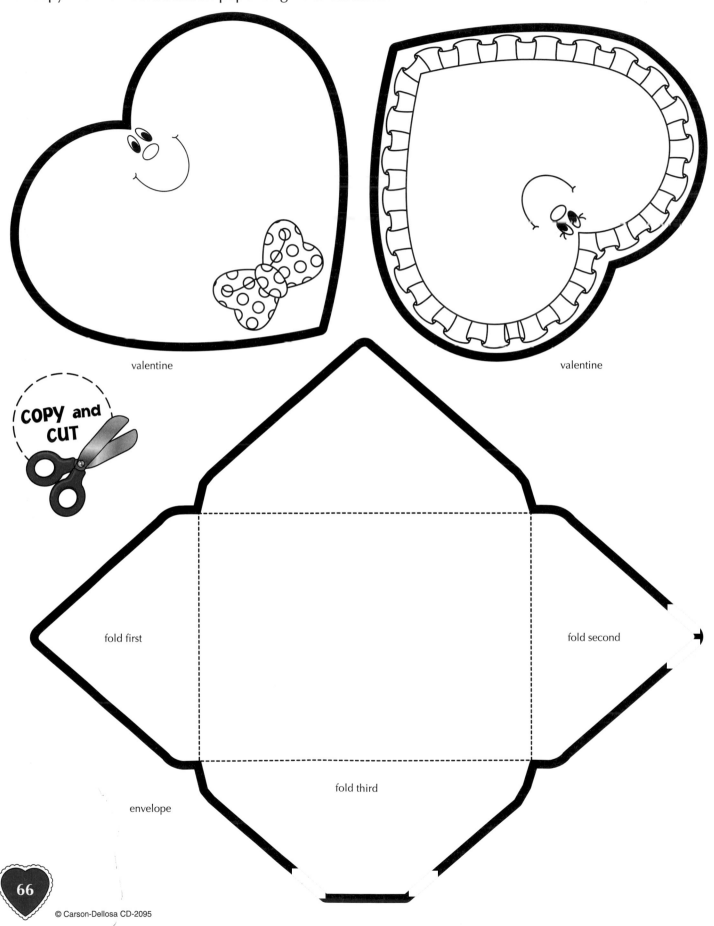

valentine

valentine

COPY and CUT

fold first

fold second

fold third

envelope

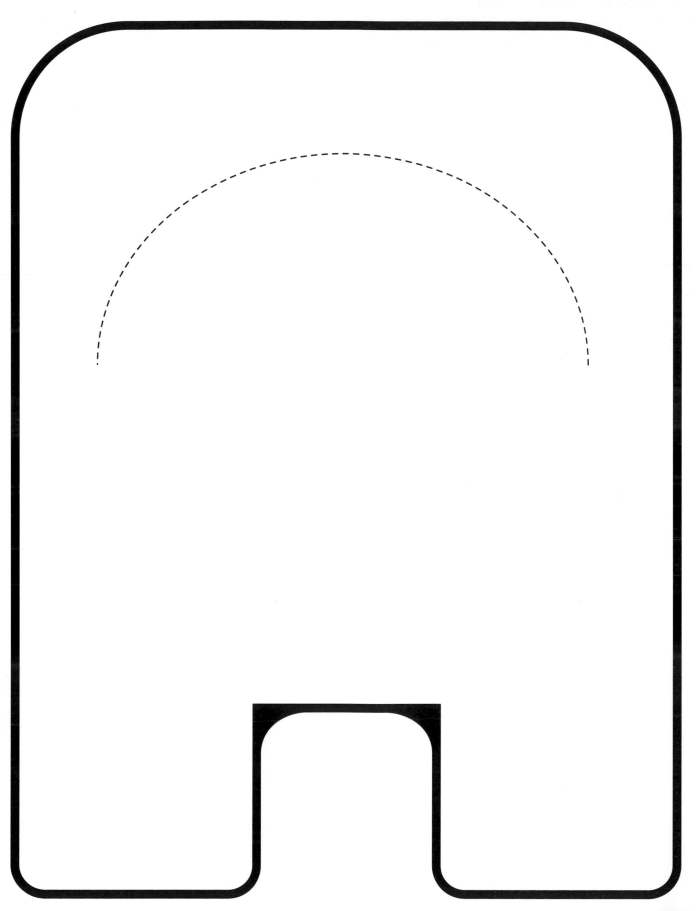

drop mailbox

Advice for Cupid

COPY and CUT

dove

cupid

(use with bulletin board idea pg. 17)

HEART SMART

Hearts are not just for Valentine's Day! February is Healthy Heart Month, a good time to teach students about this hard-working organ, and to help them learn the importance of taking care of their hearts.

Did You Know?

- ♥ In your lifetime, your heart could beat over 3 billion times.
- ♥ It takes less than a minute for a drop of blood to travel through your body and back to your heart again.
- ♥ Because your heart is so important, your body has a built in structure to protect it…your rib cage!

Literature Selections

The Heart: Our Circulatory System by Seymour Simon: Mulberry Books, 1999. (Nonfiction book, 32 pg.) A complete tour of the circulatory system with electron microscope photography.

The Heart: The Kids' Question and Answer Book by J. Willis Hurst: McGraw-Hill, 1998. (Nonfiction book, 32 pg.) Full of easy-to-understand answers about the heart, from a cardiologist.

Blood and Circulation by Jackie Hardie: Heineman Library, 1997. (Nonfiction book, 32 pg.) Complete, easy-to-understand information about the circulatory system, including heart diagrams.

A "Heart"y Muscle

Have students flex their muscles to learn how hard their hearts work for them. Explain that the heart is about the size of a fist and is mostly made of muscle cells that constantly contract and relax to pump blood through the body. The heart beats continuously, 75-85 times a minute, every minute of a person's life. Give students an idea of how much work this is by squeezing a tennis ball. Let each student try squeezing and releasing a tennis ball continuously for one minute. Challenge them to squeeze 75 times in one minute and observe how tired their hand, finger, and arm muscles become. How do our hearts manage all this work? Explain that the heart is made of strong, resilient, cardiac muscle that can work at a constant pace without getting tired.

√69√

Racing Heartbeats

Let students try to work as fast as their hearts. Divide the class into 3-4 groups. Provide each group with two large plastic dish pans, a 1-cup and a $\frac{1}{4}$-cup measuring cup, a bucket of water, and a stopwatch. Let students measure 10 cups of water (representing the amount of blood the heart pumps in 30 seconds) into one dish pan. Use the $\frac{1}{4}$-cup (representing the amount of blood the heart pumps in one beat) to transfer the water to the empty pan. Time each group to see how much water it can "pump" in 30 seconds without spilling.

Stay on the Path

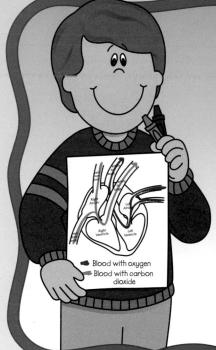

Help students learn about the circulatory system. Give each child a copy of the heart pattern (page 73). Have her trace the path of blood through the body. Starting with the veins from the body, move through the right atrium and right ventricle, to the artery to the lungs. From there, move to the veins from the lungs. Pass through the left atrium and left ventricle and exit through the artery to the body. Have students use crayons to trace the two paths and create a key, drawing a red line labeled *blood with oxygen* and a blue line labeled *blood with carbon dioxide*. Refer to the diagram at left to help students draw these paths. Explain that the heart is made up of four hollow *chambers*. The top two chambers are *atria* (singular: *atrium*), receiving blood from veins. The bottom two chambers are *ventricles*, sending blood away from the heart through arteries. Door-like *valves* connect the chambers and open and shut to let blood flow in one direction only. The heart pumps oxygenated blood to the body and blood with carbon dioxide back to the lungs, to be exhaled.

Go With the Flow

Let students make a model of the heart and follow the path of oxygen and carbon dioxide through the circulatory system. You will need 10 children, a red plastic cup, five gray paper circles labeled *carbon dioxide* (CO_2), and five white paper circles labeled *oxygen* (O_2). Choose four students to represent the four heart chambers and arrange them in the center of a room. Assign one student to be the lungs and one student to be the body. Place them about five paces from each side of the heart. Give the "lungs" the red cup and five white circles. Give the "body" the five gray circles. The remaining students will be blood vessels. Have each student wear a sign indicating the part he represents.

1. To begin, a student acting as a vein takes blood with oxygen (a red cup with a white circle in it) from the "lungs" to the student who is acting as the left atrium.
2. The left atrium student passes the cup to the left ventricle student.
3. Another student, acting as an artery, takes the cup to the "body," who removes the oxygen circle from the cup and replaces it with a carbon dioxide circle.
4. The student acting as a vein carries the cup from the "body" to the "right atrium."
5. The right atrium student passes it to the right ventricle student.
6. The last student, acting as an artery, takes the cup from the "right ventricle" to the "lungs," where that student removes the carbon dioxide circle and replaces it with an oxygen circle, completing the cycle. Repeat this activity until no circles remain, so students can see the cycle several times.

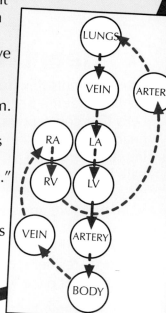

Keep the Beat

Pair students to listen to each others' heartbeats. If possible, provide stethoscopes, or make stethoscopes with funnels and plastic tubing. To make a stethoscope, fit a funnel into each end of the tubing and have one child place a funnel over his heart while the other child places a funnel over her ear. As one child listens to the other's heart, have her tap out the beat so the other child can "hear" his heart beat, too. Explain that the original stethoscope, invented in the early 1800s by Frenchman René Laënnec, was a thick tube. One end was placed over the patient's chest while the physician listened through the other end. Today, a stethoscope consists of a metal bell or disk connected to ear pieces by a plastic tube. The doctor places the metal piece over the heart. The sound of valves closing in the heart travels through the plastic tube to the ears.

Exercise Your Heart

Pulses will quicken as students learn about the benefits of exercise. Explain that a *pulse* is felt as an artery expands and contracts when the heart squeezes blood into it. Have each student locate his pulse by placing the index and middle fingers of one hand on the other wrist at the base of the thumb, feeling for vibrations. Let him count his pulse at rest for 30 seconds and record it on a Pulse Rate Log (page 73). Let students complete the exercises on the log, recording their pulses for 30 seconds after each. Let students rest between sets to return their heart rates to normal. Have them answer the questions on the log, then share their results. Explain that during exercise, the heart works faster to supply more oxygenated blood to muscles. Exercise not only makes body muscles stronger, but strengthens the heart. As a follow-up, have students brainstorm ways they can get more exercise.

Don't Chew the Fat!

Make a model of a clogged artery to help students see why they should say no to that cheeseburger! Explain that some fat is necessary for a healthy diet. However, when a person eats lots of high-fat, high-cholesterol foods, waxy deposits build up in the arteries. These deposits slow down blood and make the heart work harder to pump blood through the body. This wears out the heart and increases the risk of heart disease. Blood vessels may become completely blocked, stopping blood flow and causing a heart attack. Divide students into small groups. Have each place a funnel in a large plastic cup and record how long it takes to pour 1 cup of water through the funnel. Next, use a craft stick to clog the tip of the funnel with vegetable shortening. Poke a small hole in the shortening with a toothpick, so the funnel represents a partially clogged artery. Pour water into the funnel again. Record the time it takes to fill the cup. Ask students to compare the times, and think about how their results show the harmful effects of fatty, high cholesterol foods.

71

Feed Your Heart

Have a heart-to-heart with students about eating healthy foods. After learning what foods are bad for their hearts, challenge students to find foods that are good for their hearts. Let students look through magazines and grocery flyers and cut out pictures of heart-healthy foods such as whole grains, fruits, vegetables, low-fat proteins (chicken, fish, beans), low-fat dairy products, etc. Have each student draw and cut out a large heart shape from pink or red paper. Next, glue the pictures on the heart, covering it completely. Display the hearts with the title *Be Heart Smart*!

Nonsmoking, Please

By staging an oxygen relay race, show students that smoking is harmful to the heart. Explain that chemicals in tobacco smoke irritate artery walls, making it easier for fat and cholesterol to clog arteries. Tobacco smoke contains carbon monoxide which, when inhaled, takes up space meant for oxygen in the blood. The heart must beat faster to get enough oxygen to the body. Let students pretend to be red blood cells that must get oxygen to their bodies. Before beginning, draw two separate body outlines, one on pink paper and one on brown. Label the brown outline *Smoking* and the pink one *Nonsmoking*. Tape the outlines to a table at one end of the room. Place a large supply of white paper circles, labeled *oxygen* (O_2), and gray paper circles labeled *carbon monoxide* (CO), on a table at the other end of the room. Divide the class into two teams of "blood cells" (Smoking and Nonsmoking) and have a relay race. The object is for each team to supply their "body" with as much oxygen as possible. The Nonsmoking team may carry two oxygen circles at a time, but Smoking team members must carry one oxygen circle and one carbon monoxide circle. Have students race across the room with their circles, place them on their team's body outline, and go to the end of their lines. After everyone has had a turn, count each team's circles and compare the amount of oxygen that reached the nonsmoking body to the amount that reached the smoking body. Discuss how smoking reduces the amount of oxygen the body gets, and how much harder the heart has to work to supply the body with oxygen.

Healthy-Heart Beat-Books

The beat goes on with these heart-healthy booklets! Cut several heart shapes from red or pink paper. Stack the hearts and punch a hole in the left side. Thread a red pipe cleaner through the hole, shape it into a heart, and twist the ends together, creating a writing booklet. Challenge students to fill their books with facts about healthy heart habits, written in rhymes, raps, or poems with a beat. Let students share their books with the class.

Never smoke. Oh no way!

Eat your low in cholesterol

See your doctor every

Exercise every day.

Ginger's Heart Beat

72

PULSE RATE LOG

Activity	Pulse for 30 seconds
At rest	
March in place for 1 minute	
Run in place for 2 minutes	
At rest 3 minutes after running	

Based on the data, how does exercise affect your heart?

_____

_____

_____

_____

Why do you think exercise is good for your heart?

_____

_____

_____

_____

pulse rate log

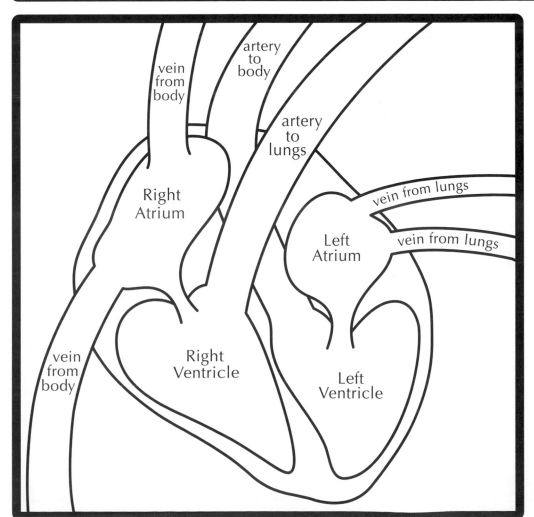

heart
(viewed from back)

COPY and CUT

THE POST OFFICE

Not only is February a great time to mail valentines, it's a great time for learning about the post office. Students can create a classroom mail center, write friendly letters, address homemade envelopes, and design their own stamps.

Did You Know?

- Benjamin Franklin was the first Postmaster General of the United States.
- In 1888, a stray dog named Owney was adopted by the Railway Mail Service. In ten years, Owney covered 143,000 miles, escorting mail deliveries across the US, Alaska, Canada, and Mexico. Owney even traveled overseas, delivering packages to China, Japan, Singapore, Algiers, and the Azores.
- In 1860-61, Pony Express riders first braved the wild west to deliver mail across the country.

Literature Selections

Mailing May by Michael O. Tunnell: Greenwillow, 1997. (Storybook, 32 pg.) Based on a true story, a girl is "mailed" to her grandmother.

Messages in the Mailbox: How to Write a Letter by Loreen Leedy: Holiday House, 1994. (Nonfiction/Picture book, 32 pg.) This introduction to letter writing includes instructions for a variety of letter styles and purposes, and addresses various aspects of correspondence.

Never Mail an Elephant by Mike Thaler: Troll Communications, 1994. (Storybook, 32 pg.) The narrator has trouble mailing an unusual birthday present.

The Post Office Book: Mail and How It Moves by Gail Gibbons: HarperCollins Children's Books, 1987. (Storybook, 32 pg.) Accessible text and well-developed illustrations provide a solid overview of postal services.

Philatelic Fun!

Encourage your students to be stamp collectors, or *philatelists* (fe•LA•te•lists). *Philately* (fe•LA•te•lee), or stamp collecting, is the most popular hobby in the world. If any students have collections, ask if they will bring them to class. For a few days, have students collect and bring stamps from home. At the end of the collection period, have students group the stamps by theme or value. Let students make booklets to sort, label, and store their stamp collections. If desired, allow students to staple waxed paper at the edge or top of each page to protect the stamps underneath.

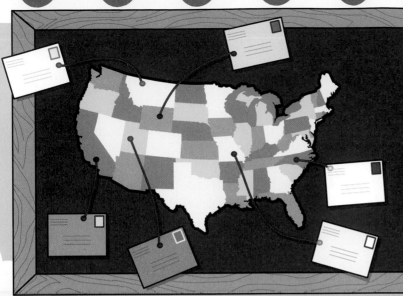

Postmark Geography

Teach geography by using a map and postmarks to help students locate places where stamps originated. Ask students to bring empty envelopes from mail received at home. Post a map on a bulletin board. As envelopes from different places arrive, staple the envelopes to the bulletin board. Mark the locations from the postmarks on the map with tacks, and run a piece of yarn or string from the origination point to the letter. Title the display *Our Mail Gets Around*.

Stamp Champs

Students will give their stamp of approval to this creative craft! Ask students to name people or objects they have seen on stamps. Explain that stamps often honor special people, things, or events. Have students think of people, objects, or events they think are special, and design stamps to honor them. Give students several enlarged copies of the postage stamp patterns (page 77) and let them design, personalize, and cut out their own series of stamps. While students are drawing, mix in a plastic tub 1/4 cup nontoxic white glue and one tablespoon of vinegar, then stir well. Next, have students paint the backs of their stamps with the glue and vinegar mixture. Place the stamps face-down to dry. To use the stamps, simply moisten the backs with water. (Nontoxic glue will not harm students who lick the stamps.) Students can use the stamps to decorate letters they send via the class mail center (see below).

A First Class Mail Center

Create your own mail center, including a central mailbox and student post office boxes. Allow a different student each week to be Postmaster, responsible for gathering mail from the classroom mailbox, sorting the notes and letters, and delivering them to the appropriate post office boxes. Encourage students to check their mailboxes daily, and to use the mail center instead of passing notes or talking during class. Use the mail center to return papers and to send your own notes to students.

To make the central mailbox, paint a large, sturdy cardboard box blue and write *Mail* in red letters on the sides. Create an access door by drawing a large square in the front, center of the box, carefully cutting along the top, left, and right edges. Cut a mail slot above the access door for students to drop in their mail.

Make students' post office boxes from a cardboard shoe organizer, adding labels to designate each student's box. You may also use thumbtacks to attach empty, square tissue boxes to a bulletin board in rows, with openings facing outward to resemble a row of post office boxes. Let students decorate and write their names on mailbox patterns (page 77), then tape them inside the shoe organizer slots or below the tissue box openings.

75

Writing Friendly Letters

Say "Write on!" to students' correspondence. Explain that a friendly letter is just that—a relaxed message between people. Ask students to decide to whom they would like to write a friendly letter. Suggest topics such as favorite school subjects, current events, funny stories, etc. Give each child two copies of the friendly letter template (page 78) and explain the parts of a friendly letter. Have each student write a rough draft of her letter on a copy of the template. Let students peer edit their letters, then write final drafts on a second copy of the template. Use *The Envelope, Please...* (below) to let students send their letters. If mailing letters is not possible, post them around the class mail center with the title *First Class Letters!*

The Envelope, Please...

Let students create and personalize their own envelopes. Give each student a sheet of paper and instruct him to hold the paper vertically. Next, have him fold the bottom five inches upward to the middle, and secure the left and right edges with tape placed edgewise across the open seams. Fold the top flap down to the center, and the envelope is ready to use! Send home an address template (page 77) with each student requesting that parents help fill out the template with the recipient's address. Have students bring the templates back and use them to address their envelopes. Next, let students attach stamps and mail their friendly letters.

Return Address Labels

Students will experience many happy returns when they make these labels! Show students examples of return address labels, then give each student 10-15 blank printer labels. Have students refer to their completed address templates (see *Writing Friendly Letters*, above) and write their address on each label. Finally, let them decorate their labels with personalized designs.

Wait a Minute, Mr. Postman!

Take time to acknowledge the people who deliver more than 630 million pieces of mail every day—our postal carriers. If possible, arrange a field trip to a nearby post office, and talk about the jobs of postal workers. Before the trip, have each student write a postcard to a family member, or bring the friendly letters they wrote during *Writing Friendly Letters* (above). At the post office, let each child buy postage for their mail and send it. You may also invite a mail carrier to visit your class to discuss his job. Before the visit, have students make up a list of questions to ask, such as *How do letters get delivered?*, *How many letters do you deliver every day?*, and *What is the Dead Letter Office?*

76

address template

_____
Sender's Name

_____
Sender's Street Address/PO Box/Apt. #

_____
Sender's City, State, Zip Code

_____
Recipient's Name

_____
Recipient's Street Address/PO Box/Apt. #

_____
Recipient's City, State, Zip Code

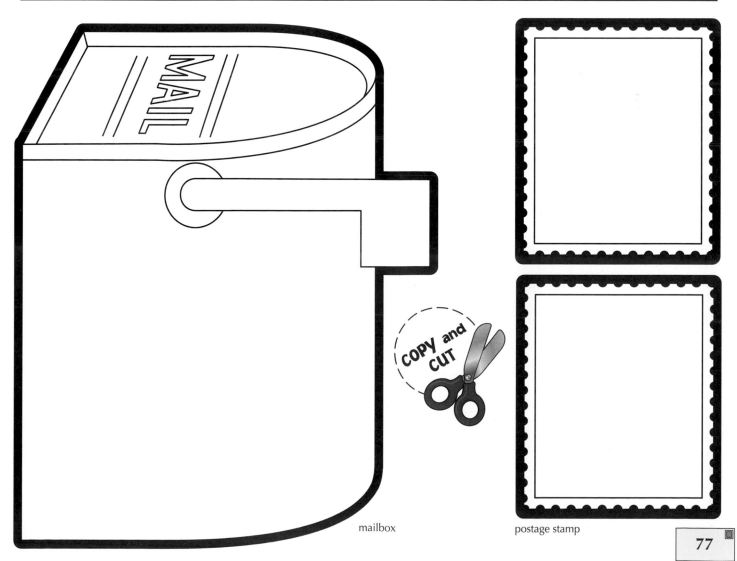

COPY and CUT

mailbox

postage stamp

77

_____

Date

_____

Greeting

_____

_____

_____

_____

_____

_____

_____

_____

_____

_____

_____

Body

_____ ,

Closing

_____

Signature

Eileen Thomas
628 Lincoln Rd.
Patterson, NC 54721

Susan Clarke
212 Windmill Dr.
Abbyton, NC 4352

John Carter
6382 Kelly Ln.
Smithville, TX 64832

Rebecca Wheeler
522 Seahawk Circle
Louise, MD 64521

Presidents' Day
Hail to the Chiefs

The third Monday in February is Presidents' Day, honoring the office of the president of the United States, as well as the birthdays of two important presidents, George Washington and Abraham Lincoln.

Did You Know?

🛡 President Richard Nixon combined Washington's and Lincoln's birthday celebrations and created one holiday, Presidents' Day, to honor all U.S. presidents.

🛡 Anyone who is a natural-born citizen of the U.S., has lived in the U.S. 14 years or longer, and is over the age of 35 can run for president!

🛡 Every president since Washington has sworn the same oath: *I do solemnly swear [or affirm] that I will faithfully execute the office of President of the United States, and will, to the best of my ability, preserve, protect, and defend the Constitution of the United States.*

Literature Selections

Ghosts of the White House by Cheryl Harness: Simon & Schuster Books for Young Readers, 1998. (Picture book, 48 pg.) Follows a girl on a school field-trip tour of the White House as she's pulled by George Washington into a painting to learn more about the house and its past inhabitants.
President Citizen by Toni Goffe: Child's Play International Ltd., 1995. (Nonfiction book, 32 pg.) Describes the principles of democracy, citizenship and the office of president.
The Story of the White House by Kate Waters: Scholastic Inc., 1992. (Nonfiction book, 40 pg.) Photos and simple text take readers on a fact-filled tour of the White House.

Presidential Portraits

Have students follow these directions to construct likenesses of Lincoln and Washington. These paper presidents can be used as report covers, decorations, or puppets in informative presidential plays.

1. Create the jacket by folding a 9" x 9" piece of construction paper (black for Lincoln, blue for Washington) at angles along the sides. Fold the top corners back to make lapels. Cut out and glue on arms and hands.
2. Cut a five-sided house-shaped "shirt" from white paper and glue it upside down between the lapels, extending slightly above the top of the jacket. Glue a head on the white tab, then draw the appropriate face.
3. To finish Washington, cut a trapezoid shape from white paper, round the corners, and glue to the back of the head to make hair. For a ruffled shirt, fold a 10" doily in half, then hold opposite edges of the semicircle and accordion fold them to meet in the center. Glue the folded doily inside the jacket, beneath the head.
4. To finish Lincoln, cut a stovepipe hat from black paper and glue it to the top of the head. Cut a bow tie from black felt. Glue it to the shirt inside the jacket. Cut a high, thin U-shape from black felt (thicker at the bottom than on the sides) and glue it to the lower face to make Lincoln's beard.

(79)

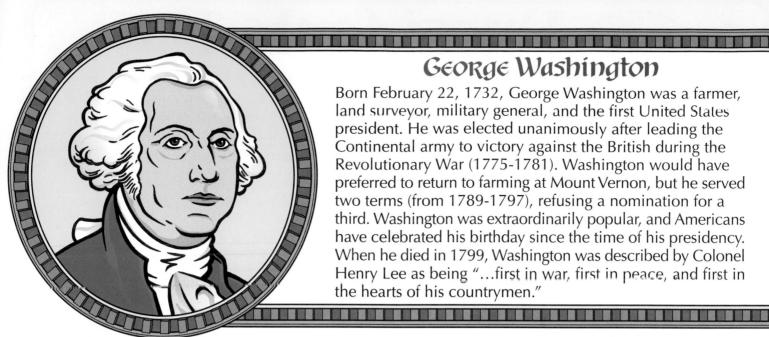

George Washington

Born February 22, 1732, George Washington was a farmer, land surveyor, military general, and the first United States president. He was elected unanimously after leading the Continental army to victory against the British during the Revolutionary War (1775-1781). Washington would have preferred to return to farming at Mount Vernon, but he served two terms (from 1789-1797), refusing a nomination for a third. Washington was extraordinarily popular, and Americans have celebrated his birthday since the time of his presidency. When he died in 1799, Washington was described by Colonel Henry Lee as being "…first in war, first in peace, and first in the hearts of his countrymen."

Did You Know?

- Washington, D.C., the capitol of the United States, is named for George Washington because he chose the site. Washington is, however, the only president never to reside in the White House.
- Contrary to popular belief, Washington did not wear a wig. Instead, he powdered his hair, as was the fashion of the time.
- Washington did have false teeth, but they were made of ivory, not wood.

Literature Selections

George Washington by Ingri and Edgar D'Aulaire: Beautiful Feet Books, 1996. (Nonfiction book, 60 pg.) A beautifully illustrated biography.
George Washington: A Picture Book Biography by James Cross Giblin: Scholastic, 1998. (Nonfiction book, 100 pg.) A complete biography with oil paintings.
George Washington's Breakfast by Jean Fritz: Paper Star, 1998. (Storybook, 48 pg.) A boy named for the first president wants to be just like him, including eating what Washington ate for breakfast.

Dollar Biography

George Washington's portrait appears on the front of the U.S. one dollar bill. Let students learn about Washington's life by making dollar bill biographies. Enlarge the dollar pattern (page 85) and have students draw pictures of Washington in the center circles of the patterns. Have students research Washington's life. Then, let the children write facts about Washington, such as his birth and death dates, on the patterns in place of the words and numbers usually found on the dollar bill. Finally, have students design their own reverse sides of the bills, including additional biographical information and illustrations.

(80)

Chop the Cherry Tree

In 1806, Mason Weems wrote a biography of Washington, including a fictional story about young George chopping down a cherry tree and confessing to his father, "I cannot tell a lie. I did it with my hatchet." Let students chop down cherry trees to reveal tales about good character. Cut a tree trunk from brown paper and a treetop from green paper. Glue the treetop to the trunk, then cut the trunk in half. Glue the bottom of the trunk to construction paper. Reattach the treetop to the paper with a paper fastener, aligning the two parts. Draw and cut out an ax. Attach it to the paper with a second fastener, so the ax blade swings to meet the trunk. Trace the treetop shape on the underlying construction paper, then slide the treetop to the side. Have each student write a character-oriented story on the construction paper, within the outline. Slide the ax to chop the tree. Slide the treetop to reveal the story underneath.

Rules of Civility

As a child, George Washington practiced his handwriting by copying rules for social graces and good behavior from a book called *The Rules of Civility* (republished by Beaver Press, 1971). Read aloud some of the rules Washington copied (below). Have students paraphrase these rules, or brainstorm new rules of civility for modern times. After creating the list, have each child copy it in his best handwriting.

Rules of Civility

★ Every action done in company ought to be with some sign of respect to those that are present.

★ In the presence of others, sing not to yourself with a humming noise, nor drum with your fingers, or feet.

★ Turn not your back to others, especially in speaking; jog not the table or desk on which another reads or writes; lean not upon any one.

★ Do not laugh too loud or too much at any public spectacle.

★ Drink not, nor talk with your mouth full; neither gaze about you while you are drinking.

Class Constitution

The United States Constitution was written in 1789 to establish a form for the U.S. government and ensure rights for its people. Washington presided over the Constitutional Convention in 1789, and was the first to sign the Constitution. Write the preamble to the Constitution on an overhead projector. Read it aloud with students. Next, reword the preamble to fit your classroom. Divide students into seven groups, and have each write an article for the class constitution. Allow every child to sign the constitution, then post it in the classroom.

We the students of Ms. Stradley's class, in order to form a more perfect Classroom, establish fairness, ensure friendliness, provide for conflict resolution, promote learning, and secure happiness for ourselves and our school, do ordain and establish this Constitution for Ms. Stradley's class.

Hank   Tara   Wolf   Joey   Britney
Kelly   AMBER   Maria   Kim   Dez   Julie
Jeff   Jennifer   Carol   Erin   Tracy   Alain

81

Abraham Lincoln

Born in Kentucky on February 12, 1809, Abraham Lincoln was the sixteenth U.S. president. Lincoln grew up in a log cabin in Indiana, teaching himself writing and math. He loved reading, and walked long distances to borrow books. As a young man, Lincoln earned money by splitting logs, but eventually became a lawyer. Lincoln, who was president during the Civil War, is remembered for keeping the Union together and for issuing the Emancipation Proclamation which abolished slavery. Some people did not agree with Lincoln's beliefs, and on April 15, 1865, Lincoln was shot and killed while attending a play at Ford's Theatre in Washington, D.C., only days after the Civil War ended.

Did You Know?

- Abraham Lincoln owned a dog named Jib, a cat named Bob, and a turkey named Jack.
- In 1860, a 13-year-old named Thomas Alva Edison sold presidential campaign posters of Abraham Lincoln.
- While campaigning for president, Lincoln received a letter from an 11-year-old girl, Grace Bidwell, suggesting he might have a better chance of winning the election if he grew a beard. Lincoln took her advice, and he won the election.

Literature Selections

Abe Lincoln's Hat by Martha Brenner: Random House, Inc., 1994. (Nonfiction book, 48 pg.) An easy-reader about a unique practice of Lincoln's—keeping letters in his stovepipe hat.

Honest Abe by Edith I. Kunhardt: Morrow, William, & Co., 1993. (Nonfiction book, 32 pg.) Colorful folk art illustrations accompany a simple biography of Lincoln.

Where Lincoln Walked by Raymond Bial: Walker & Co., 1997. (Nonfiction book, 48 pg.) Photographs take the reader on a virtual tour of historical sites related to the sixteenth U.S. president.

Stovepipe Hat Biography

What's inside Lincoln's hat? His biography! As postmaster of New Salem, Illinois, Lincoln was known to put letters inside his tall, black hat so he would not misplace them. Have students write biographies of Lincoln and store them in a stovepipe hat. Give each child an 8" x 10" piece of oaktag and two pieces of 9" x 12" black paper. Fold a 1" tab along the two short ends of one of the black papers, roll it into a half-cylinder, then glue the tabs to the oaktag. Cut an 8" diameter circle from the other black paper. Place the half-cylinder on top of the circle to create the hat's brim. Fold up the half-circle behind the oaktag and secure it to the back with glue. Tape the hat to the brim inside the half-cylinder. Have students write their names and a biography title on the oaktag along the sides of the hat. Let them decorate the crafts with pennies and biographical illustrations. Staple the biographies to a bulletin board or stand them up along a bookshelf.

Log Cabins

Lincoln grew up in a one-room log cabin with a dirt floor and a stone fireplace. His chores consisted of fetching water, gathering firewood, and working in the fields, but he always made time for learning. Read to students about Lincoln's childhood, then make log cabins that show how Lincoln spent his youth. Have each child stuff a lunch-sized brown paper bag with crumpled paper, so it stands up. Fold and staple the bag's top. Cut out an 8" x 5" piece of brown or black paper, fold it in half, and glue it to the top of the bag for a roof. Next, glue craft sticks along the two longer sides of the bag to resemble split logs. On small paper squares, have students draw pictures of young Abe reading, writing, building a fire, etc. Glue the drawings to the bag, creating cabin "windows." Let students finish their cabins by adding doors and chimneys.

Speech, Speech!

In 1863, Lincoln gave a speech at a Civil War battlefield in Gettysburg, Pennsylvania, where many people died. His speech was short, and people at the time did not think much of it. Today, however, Lincoln's Gettysburg Address is recognized as one of the most important speeches in American history. Read the Gettysburg Address to students, then discuss it. Talk about what Lincoln meant by a government "of the people, by the people, for the people." Next, encourage students to choose a Presidents' Day related topic, such as *Which presidents should be on coins and paper money*, or, *Things the president should do for children*, and compose a short speech to give to the class. Remind students to choose their words carefully. If desired, allow students to mail their speeches to: The President, c/o the Office of Presidential Student Correspondence, The White House, 1600 Pennsylvania Avenue, Washington, D.C. 20500.

Coin Flip Book

Make double-sided penny booklets that are heads (and tails!) above the rest. Have each child cut out four 6" circles, two from orange paper and two from notebook paper. Have students staple the papers together on the left side to make a booklet, using the orange papers as covers. Instruct each student to use a brown or gold crayon to draw the "head" of the penny on one orange circle, then flip the booklet over so the staple is still on the left side, and draw the "tail" of the penny. Next, have students research facts about pennies and the Lincoln Memorial. Orienting the booklets to the "head" side, have students write facts about pennies on the front of each page. Next, flip the coin booklet over so that the Lincoln Memorial is right side up. Write facts about the Lincoln Memorial on the front of these pages.

More About the Presidents

Hang Your Hats

Teach students about the president's duties by examining the many hats he wears. Give students enlarged copies of presidential hat patterns (page 86). Have them trace the edge of each hat with a crayon, adding color and small details. Instruct students to label each hat with a job the president has—military hat: Commander in Chief; election hat: Leader of the Party; three-cornered hat: Chief Executive; top hat (stovepipe hat): Chief of State; Uncle Sam hat: Leader of the Nation. Provide reference books describing the jobs of the president, then have students write on each pattern details of what the president does for each job. Punch a hole in the corner of each hat and tie them together with a loop of yarn. Hang the hats with push pins on a bulletin board with the title, *The Many Hats the President Wears*.

Windows on the White House

The White House
by Hank R.

Help students learn about the White House, home of the president of the United States since 1800, as they complete this interactive picture activity. Enlarge the White House pattern (page 85) for each student. Have her cut along three sides of several windows to make flaps. For younger students, two windows may need to be cut as one flap. Place another sheet of paper behind the pattern and tape the edges. Have students write facts about the White House under each flap. Younger students can draw pictures of rooms and objects in the White House. Let students complete their pictures by coloring the flag, sky, grass, flowers, etc.

Monumental Biographies

Transport students to the Black Hills of South Dakota with these presidential biographies "carved" out of paper. Have each student chose a different U.S. president and write a short report on an index card. Instruct each child to draw a pencil sketch bust of the president on off-white construction paper, filling up as much of the paper as possible. Then, have students cut around the outline of their drawings. Cover a bulletin board with light blue paper. Staple a larger piece of off-white paper, cut to look like rocks, across the bottom of the board to create a mountain. Stagger the busts across the "rocks" to create a new Mount Rushmore. Display the reports along with their "carved" images.

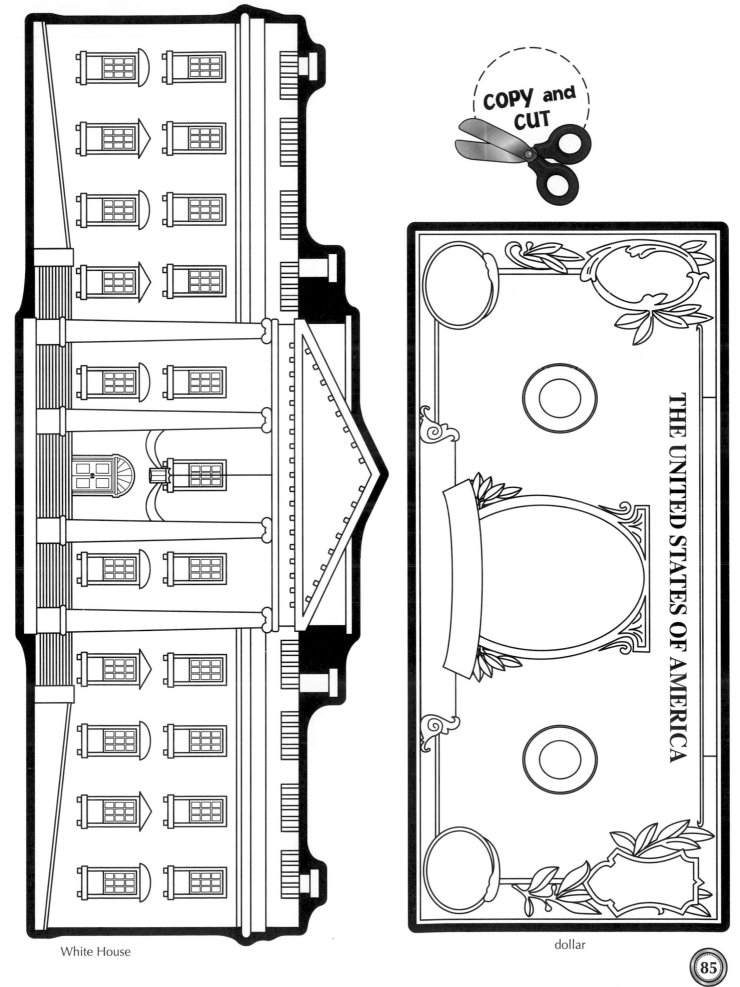

COPY and CUT

THE UNITED STATES OF AMERICA

White House

dollar

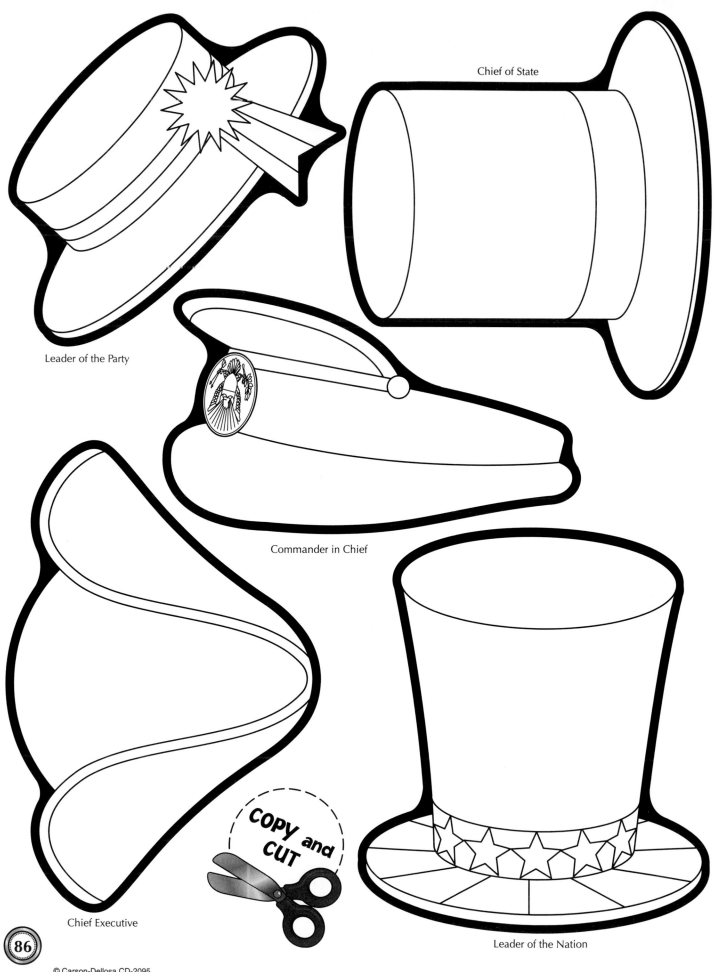

Chief of State

Leader of the Party

Commander in Chief

Chief Executive

COPY and CUT

Leader of the Nation

Pets and Pet Care
Fur, Feathers, Paws, and Claws
February is Responsible Pet Owner Month—the "purr-fect" time to teach students the responsibilities of caring for a pet.

Did You Know?
- The ancient Egyptians considered cats to be the most sacred of animals. They also kept pet dogs, which looked a lot like greyhounds.
- Hospitals and convalescent centers sometimes bring cats, dogs, birds, and fish to visit with patients and help them feel better.
- Just like people, dogs and cats are either left- or right-"handed."

Literature Selections
Pet Show by Ezra Jack Keats: Simon & Schuster, 1974. (Picture book, 32 pg.)
Archie can't find his cat to enter it in the neighborhood pet show.
Weird Pet Poems compiled by Dilys Evans: Simon & Schuster, 1997. (Poetry book, 38 pg.)
A story that incorporates poems by Karla Kuskin, May Swenson, Theodore Roethke, and others.
Daddy, Could I Have an Elephant? by Jake Wolf: Greenwillow Books, 1996. (Picture book, 32 pg.)
Humorous illustrations accompany this lighthearted story about a child's wish for various pets.

Pet Project

Feed pets' needs! Kick off your pet care lesson by helping students learn what kinds of attention different pets need. Use an overhead projector to enlarge each of the pet patterns (pages 90-92). Divide students into six groups. Give each group a pattern to color lightly with crayons. Provide reference materials and ask each group to identify the kind of care their pet needs, for example, exercise, fish flakes, a cage, etc. Let groups write the pet's needs on their patterns. Next, provide pet supply catalogs and magazines and have each group decorate its pattern with pictures of the needed supplies. On a bulletin board, create a pet store window and hang the decorated patterns on the display. If desired, have students use catalogs and flyers to total the costs of the required supplies. Post sums beside the patterns to see how much each pet would cost. Finally, let each group share its information and talk about what all pets need: lots of love!

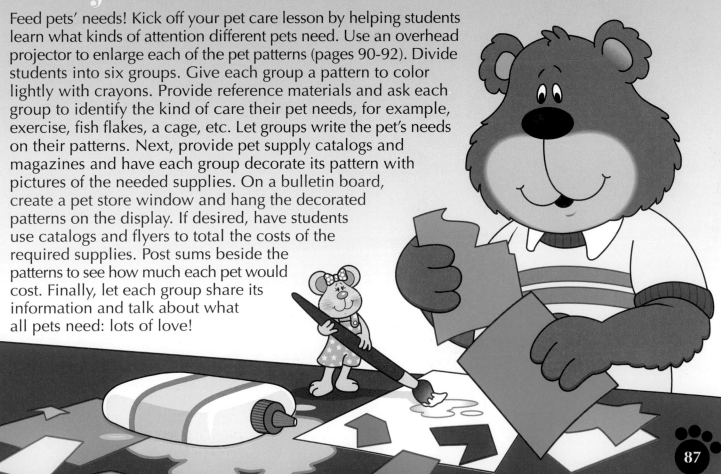

87

Pet Portraits

Let students picture themselves with their favorite animal friends. Give each student a 5¹/₂" x 5¹/₂" piece of paper, crayons, and markers. Have her draw a picture of herself with her own pet or with a pet she would like to own. When the pictures are complete, glue poster board or cardboard strips around the pictures to create frames. Then, have students draw and cut out pet toys, paw prints, treats, etc., to glue around their frames. If desired, real treats and toys can be used to decorate the frames. Tape a loop of yarn to the back of each picture and hang them in a special place in the classroom.

Plush Pet Show

What kind of animals are easy to care for? Stuffed animals! Have each student bring in a stuffed animal from home. Provide construction paper for students to make identification tags for their pretend pets. The pet's name and the owner's name should appear on each tag. Have each student punch a hole in the identification tag, thread yarn through it, and tie the tag around his stuffed animal's neck. Plan a class pet show where each student can introduce his pet and talk about it. Give each pet an award for being the fluffiest, softest, oldest, etc. If desired, group pets according to type, size, color, texture, etc.

Bathe the Toucan

Imaginations are sure to run wild when students write these mismatched pet care stories. Write pet care actions such as *walk, brush/groom, bathe, feed,* etc., on pet patterns (pages 90-92). Fold the patterns and put them in a bowl. In another bowl, place pet patterns with names of exotic animals such as iguanas, tarantulas, snakes, potbellied pigs, etc. Let each student choose a pattern from each bowl, then write and illustrate a story based on the action and the chosen animal. For instance, she may write a story about bathing a toucan, walking a snake, or brushing an iguana! Let students share their stories with the class before displaying them on a bulletin board titled *Wacky Pet Care Stories!*

Not Just the Teacher's Pet

A class pet is more than just a companion, it is a real live learning opportunity for students. Following is a list of activities for students to complete with their class pet.

- 🐾 Have students learn more about the class pet. Is it a nocturnal animal? What is its natural habitat? What does it eat in the wild? What kind of home or nest does it build?
- 🐾 Have students observe the class pet and record what it does at various times of the day. When is it most active? How much food and water does it consume? If the pet sleeps most of the day, have students look for clues in its cage that may help them figure out what the animal does during the night.
- 🐾 Let your pet travel! Arrange for several responsible students to take the pet to visit other classrooms. Ask for student volunteers to take the pet over weekends and school vacations. Send a scrapbook in which students can write and draw pictures about special adventures the pet had during its travels.

Pet Treats

Make pets' mouths water with these scrumptious dog and cat treats.

Ingredients:
2 cups whole wheat flour
$\frac{1}{2}$ cup cornmeal
$\frac{2}{3}$ cup water
6 tablespoons oil

Mix all ingredients together. Cut into large shapes (such as bones) for dogs, and small shapes (such as fish) for cats. Bake at 350° for 35-40 minutes.

After the treats are complete, let students decorate small lunch bags to resemble cats and dogs, then put several treats in each bag. Staple the top of the bag closed. Let students take their treats home to their pets, or donate the treats to a local animal shelter.

Adopt-a-Pet

Give a pretend animal a home with this class pet adoption activity. Bring a stuffed animal to class and place it in a travel bag. Include a bound journal with approximately 30 pages. Allow students to take turns "adopting" the animal for a night. Have each child write a journal entry from the animal's perspective, recording where it went, what the student and animal did together, and so on. When the pet has visited each student's home, display the journal or have students read their entries to the class.

89

fish

COPY and CUT

rabbit

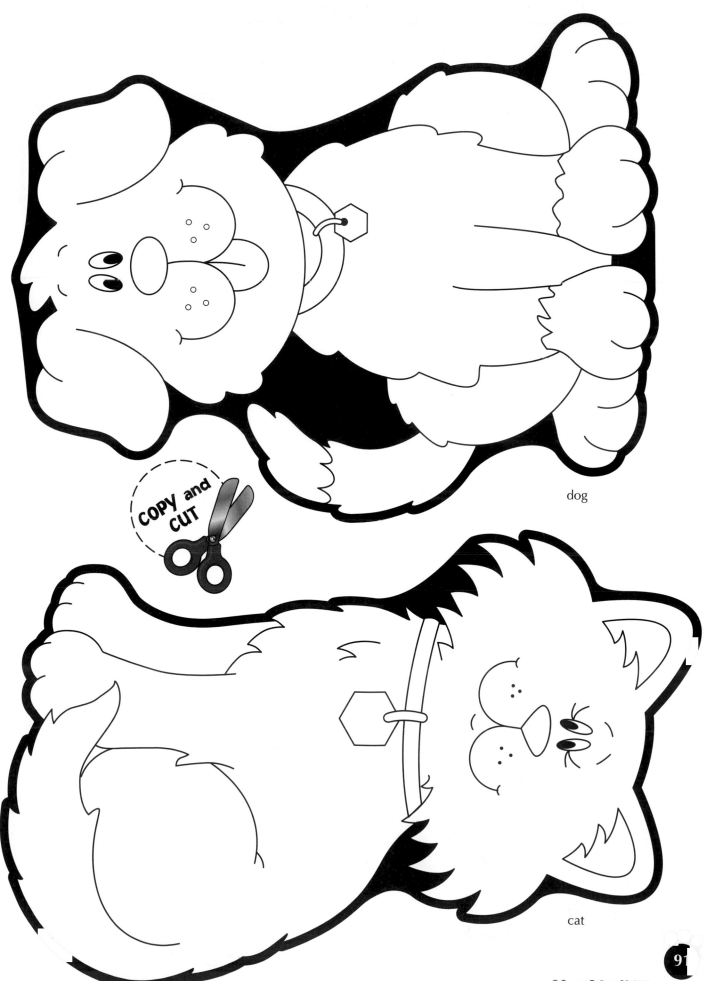

COPY and CUT

dog

cat

COPY and CUT

hamster

bird

INTERNATIONAL
Holidays

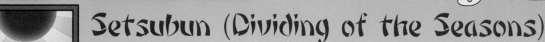

Setsubun (Dividing of the Seasons)

According to the Japanese calendar, Setsubun (SAYT•zoo•boon) is the last day before spring arrives! Every February 3 or 4, Japanese families gather to drive away bad luck and to ensure good fortune for the year. Participants shout "Oni wa soto! Fuku wa uchi!" (OH•nee wa SO•toe FOO•koo wa OO•chee) meaning "Out with goblins! In with luck!" Children make goblin masks and attend elaborate ceremonies at temples and shrines.

Oni Masks

Oni (OH•nee) are well-known Japanese goblins with horns and red or blue faces. One tradition is called *mame-maki* (MAH•may MAH•kee), or the bean-throwing ceremony. Children run around chasing adults dressed as oni, throwing lucky dried soybeans called *fuku-mame* (FOO•koo MAH•may) at them. Let students make their own oni masks by drawing goblin faces on construction paper. Cut out eye, nose, and mouth holes, and add construction paper accents and ornaments. Secure the masks by punching holes in the sides and threading string or elastic through the holes. Let students wear their masks during the activities below.

Mame-maki Bean Bags

Students can use lucky bean bags to perform their own bean-throwing ceremony. To make bean bags, give each student a 6" x 12" piece of fabric and some dried beans. Fold the fabric in half to form a square, then place the beans inside the fold. Glue the three remaining edges closed and allow the glue to dry. Next, divide the class into groups and play "Hot Potato" with a Setsubun twist. Let students wear their oni masks and sit in a circle. Play Japanese music while each group passes around a bean bag. When the music stops, the "oni" caught with the bean bag is out. Continue until there is one oni left in each group. These oni are the winners!

Fuku-mame Math

Japanese tradition says that to guarantee health and fortune in the coming year, Setsubun participants should eat the number of fuku-mame beans equal to their age. Use this tradition to reinforce basic math concepts. Provide roasted soybeans or peanuts and let each student count and eat a number of beans equal to her age. Ask students to determine how many beans each row, table, group, or the entire class would eat. Have students create graphs indicating parents', students', and friends' ages by gluing soybeans to construction paper.

Carnival (Lent Celebration)

A derivative of an early 17th century Portuguese Lent commemoration, Carnival was brought to Brazil by colonists and is now a spectacular, widely celebrated holiday. In Rio de Janeiro, for the four days before Ash Wednesday, tens of thousands of people gather to celebrate Carnival with huge parades, elaborate floats and costumes, live music, and samba dancing.

School Spirit!

How do you get into the Carnival parade? Go to school! Regional dance clubs called *samba schools* compete for the right to march on parade days. Each samba school has its own colors, theme, and flag, and their choreographed dances tell stories based on Brazilian history and folklore. Allow students to form their own samba schools in groups of five or six. (Note that students will work with and participate in these groups for the activities on pages 94-95.) Ask each group to choose a name, an accompanying theme, and school colors, based upon some aspect of Brazilian history, culture, or folklore. Next, have students create a flag to carry in their class Carnival parade (*Parade*, p. 95) that incorporates their samba school's theme and colors. Give each group a large rectangle of butcher paper and let them use paint, crayons, markers, and construction paper shapes to create a flag. Encourage students to be creative and use elaborate, colorful designs.

Carnival Crafts

After students have chosen their themes and created their flags, it is time to complete the other items needed to participate in a Carnival parade—drums and fancy headdresses!

Headdresses

Make headdresses by cutting a wide strip of sturdy paper the diameter of each student's head. Tape the ends together so the strip fits snugly. Use this strip as the base for attaching feathers, glitter, sequins, and other theme-related cut-outs such as wings, fruit, flowers, cones, and stars. Let students decorate the headdresses like the flags—extravagantly!

Drums

Hand-played drums can be made from clean, empty household objects such as coffee cans, oatmeal containers, and plastic storage bowls. Decorate the drums with foil, construction paper, yarn, glitter, paint, etc.

Everybody, Samba!

Samba is a complex, rhythmic, improvisational style of music and dance closely associated with Carnival. It grew out of the mix of African, Portuguese, and local traditional music of Rio. Have each group choreograph a one- or two-minute performance based on their samba school's chosen theme. Ask drummers to compose and play a rhythm while dancers choreograph a theme-based dance.

Samba Music

Look for music by samba artists such as Antonio Carlos Jobim, Joao Gilberto, Beth Carvalho, and Gilberto Gil, or play these compilations of samba music for your class:

Brasil: Samba De Carnaval, Laserlight, 1991, compact audio disk.
Samba Brazil, Uni/Verve, 1992, compact audio disk.

Concentration

The gathering of participants before the Carnival parade is known as the *concentration*. Let your students hold their own concentration, selecting their roles and places in the upcoming parade. Allow students to choose their parade roles, such as samba dancers, drummers, and flag bearers. Flag bearers usually head up Carnival parades, accompanied by special dancing escorts. The main group of samba dancers follows. The drummers, setting the pace and keeping the rhythm, round out the procession. Encourage students to expand these roles or invent new ones to fit their themes. For example, a group researching Carmen Miranda may want to include students dressed as the flamboyant Brazilian performer. A group researching samba music may wish to represent Tia Ciata, one of the musicians who developed the samba.

Parade

Only the best samba schools make it to the Carnival parades in Rio, which include thousands of samba dancers in costumes, drummers, floats, and each school's flag bearers. When students' preparations are complete, it is time for their Carnival parade! If desired, let your students perform for another class or for parents, or let groups take turn watching their classmates' parades!

FOOD

Carnival Foods

After the parades, allow students to relax and celebrate their successful performances with a variety of traditional Carnival foods and drinks. Popular snacks include pineapple, guava fruit, and popcorn (colored, if possible). Coconut milk, pineapple juice, and other tropical fruit juices are popular beverage options.

PINK POPCORN
PIPOCAS

N'CWALA (FIRST FRUIT CEREMONY)

In 1835, Ngoni tribesmen crossed the Zambezi River into what is now Zambia, Africa. Their celebration of this event coincided with a total eclipse of the sun. Since that time, the Ngoni have regarded February 24 as a time for all 12 tribes to gather and give thanks for their good fortune. The highlight of this holiday, N'cwala, is the tasting of the year's first fresh produce by the Paramount Chief of the Ngoni. During this time, the gathered tribes celebrate with dancing, drumming, and feasting.

Rites of Passage

The Ngoni are considered southern Africa's best dancers, and local chiefs bring their best dancers to the N'cwala celebration. Because great dancers are considered strong protectors of the chief, tribesmen display their prowess with a stick called a *N'kholi* and a small shield called a *chishango*. Students can make N'kholi by rolling an 11" x 17" sheet of paper lengthwise into a tight tube and securing the seam with tape. To make the chishango, let students decorate the bottom of a paper plate with African animal fur patterns such as zebra stripes or leopard spots. Next, have students secure a dowel rod, unsharpened pencil, or craft stick handle to the inner (top) side of the plate. Attach the handle with tape, or thread it through holes cut into the top and bottom of the plate. Now, students are ready to dance! (See *The N'cwala Dance,* below.)

The N'cwala Dance

Let your students display their dancing prowess using their new crafts. Have students make a circle, with their chishango in their left hands, and their N'kholi in their right hands, then teach them this dance.

Lift your right knee, raise your right hand up above your head, and extend your left hand in front of you.

Then, stamp your right foot and bring your arms in close to your body.

Next, raise your left knee and right hand, while extending your left hand.

Stamp your left foot and bring your arms in again, then repeat the steps while moving forward around the circle.

Allow several students to clap out a rhythm while others dance.